Architectural Design
November/December 2006

Architextiles

Guest-edited by
Mark Garcia

D0872768

WILEY-ACADEMY

ISBN-13 9780470026342
ISBN-10 0470026340
Profile No 184
Vol 76 No 6

Editorial Offices
International House
Ealing Broadway Centre
London W5 5DB

T: +44 (0)20 8326 3800
F: +44 (0)20 8326 3801
E: architecturaldesign@wiley.co.uk

Editor
Helen Castle

Production Controller
Jenna Brown

Project Management
Caroline Ellerby

Design and Prepress
Artmedia Press, London

Printed in Italy by Conti Tipocolor

Advertisement Sales
Faith Pidduck/Wayne Frost
T +44 (0)1243 770254
E fpidduck@wiley.co.uk

Front cover: DR_D Lab (Art Academy Stuttgart), The Living Museum: Pimp My Architecture, 2005. © Dagmar Richter

Requests to the Publisher should be addressed to:
Permissions Department,
John Wiley & Sons Ltd,
The Atrium
Southern Gate
Chichester,
West Sussex PO19 8SQ
England

F: +44 (0)1243 770571
E: permreq@wiley.co.uk

Subscription Offices UK
John Wiley & Sons Ltd
Journals Administration Department
1 Oldlands Way, Bognor Regis
West Sussex, PO22 9SA
T: +44 (0)1243 843272
F: +44 (0)1243 843232
E: cs-journals@wiley.co.uk

[ISSN: 0003-8504]

AD is published bimonthly and is available to purchase on both a subscription basis and as individual volumes at the following prices.

Single Issues
Single issues UK: £22.99
Single issues outside UK: US$45.00
Details of postage and packing charges available on request.

Annual Subscription Rates 2006
Institutional Rate
Print only or Online only: UK£175/US$290
Combined Print and Online: UK£193/US$320
Personal Rate
Print only: UK£99/US$155
Student Rate
Print only: UK£70/US$110
Prices are for six issues and include postage and handling charges. Periodicals postage paid at Jamaica, NY 11431. Air freight and mailing in the USA by Publications Expediting Services Inc, 200 Meacham Avenue, Elmont, NY 11003
Individual rate subscriptions must be paid by personal cheque or credit card. Individual rate subscriptions may not be resold or used as library copies.

All prices are subject to change without notice.

Postmaster
Send address changes to 3 Publications Expediting Services, 200 Meacham Avenue, Elmont, NY 11003

C O N T E N T S

AD

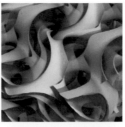

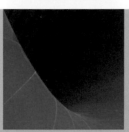

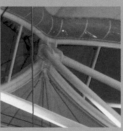

Λ\D+

Editorial

A flick through this issue confounds expectations. Synthetic meshed landscapes, computed curves, high-performance textiles, ETFE panels and biotissues hobnob with sandbags, 'crinolines', veils, screens, sculpted pods and surface patterning. Whereas once the fabric in architecture formed a discrete body of work under the leading light of the German architect Frei Otto – characterised by highly engineered and refined tensile membranes – *Architextiles* is a rich 'ragbag'. It represents a whole new enthusiasm for the textile in architecture, which is simultaneously sensual and technically charged. It is catholic rather than dogmatic in its definition of what the 'architextile' might be, emphasising materials and techniques that are textile in character, but not mutually so. For, as explained by Marie O'Mahony in 'Textiles for 21st-Century Living' (pp 102–7), the current trend in textiles is towards the blending of materials, the application of textile techniques with nontextiles and general hybridisation. Similarly, this title of *AD* encompasses contributors and architects who have a long experience and knowledge of textiles as well as those who have come afresh to the subject. It features those such as Robert Kronenburg, who has been one of the chief advocates of portable, inflatable and fabric structures, and Dominique Perrault, who has been researching the relationship between architecture and textiles for 16 years, alongside Will Alsop who, after a brief fling with textiles in his student days at the Architectural Association (AA), is only now fully rediscovering the sculptural potential of fabric structures.

To allude to this publication as a 'ragbag' is to deny the rigorous thinking that underlies it. Mark Garcia has taken his subject and not only collected an extremely exciting body of work, but also invited leaders in their field to shed light on the most important aspects. These include the likes of Matilda McQuaid, curator of the 'Extremes Textiles' exhibition (April to October 2005) at the Cooper-Hewitt Museum in New York, discussing high-performance textiles, David Wakefield of specialist consultancy Tensys giving the whys and wherefores of tensile structure design, and members of Arup's Advanced Geometry Unit discussing their cutting-edge research in this field. The generative design preoccupations of some of the most exciting designers are explored with close-ups on the work and thinking of Will Alsop, Nigel Coates, Dominique Perrault and Lars Spuybroek. These longer articles are effectively punctuated by projects that provide yet another glimpse of what an architextile might be, whether it is the 'great veil' of Massimiliano Fuksas's New Trade Fair in Milan or Jane Rendell's Purdah embellishment on a gallery window. Garcia's issue is a truly decorative weave, pulling together a rich and diverse body of work with an underlying structure. Δ   *Helen Castle*

David LaChapelle, 'My House',
Alek Wek in Christian Lacroix,
New York, *Paris Vogue*, 1997.

Architecture + Textiles = Architextiles

A hybrid term, 'architextiles' encompasses a wide range of projects and ways of thinking that unite architecture and textiles. By way of introduction to this issue, guest-editor **Mark Garcia** highlights the significant rise of interest in this confluence by theorists, architects, engineers, textile designers, materials scientists and artists. He also explains how, as a hybrid mode of design and practice, architextiles is better able to respond to society's fast-changing cultural and consumer demands, enabling the production of more dynamic, flexible, interactive, event and process-based spaces.

Mina Tent City, Saudi Arabia, 1997
This vast permanent city of 57,000 PTFE-coated fibreglass, air-conditioned tents was built to accommodate 1.5 million Hajj pilgrims. The city is divided up into 'countries', with flags representing the nationality of each section.

A new generation of giant-scale textiles is at the core of a revolution in architecture.

S Hanna and PA Beasley[1]

According to Kurt Forster, art and architecture first intersected when man learned to fasten a textile to a post.[2] Closer to our own times, the first marks made by man on the surface of Mars were imprints of the textile landing airbags deployed by the NASA *Pathfinder* mission in 1997–98. These two events mark extreme poles of a continuous history of intimate exchange between architecture[3] and textile design. Between these two events is a long and largely uncharted history of productive multidisciplinary cross-fertilisations and research, and recent signs suggest that the consilience between architecture and textiles is intensifying.

Significant, recently built examples of this include projects such as Murphy Jahn's Bangkok International Airport (2006), Nicholas Grimshaw's Space Centre Rocket Tower in Leicester (2001) and Richard Rogers' Millennium Dome, London (1999). In addition, the popularity and appearance in quick succession of books like Bradley Quinn's *The Fashion of Architecture*[4] and Marie O'Mahony and Sarah Braddock Clarke's *Techno Textiles*,[5]

and exhibitions such as 'Extreme Textiles' at the Cooper-Hewitt, New York (2005) and 'Skin and Bones' at the Museum of Contemporary Art, Los Angeles (2006–07), are symptomatic of the growing importance of what Lars Spuybroek has described as a 'textile way of thinking' in architecture. This way of thinking and making has a long and winding, but largely neglected history that has only recently witnessed a significant rise in interest from theorists, architects, engineers, textile designers, materials scientists and artists. Its history is sewn into our everyday language.

Etymologies and Definitions of Architextiles

The etymological link is explicit. 'Textile', 'technology', 'text', 'texture', 'connection' and 'context' are all derivative inflections of the same proto-Indo-European word *'tek'*, which is the root of 'architecture'. 'Technology' and 'textile' are also both derived from the Latin *'texere'*, meaning to weave, connect and/or construct. 'Fabric' has its origins in the Latin *'fabricare'*, or *'fabre'*, meaning to work, or to make. Architectural parlance contains more examples, such as urban fabric, curtain wall, ribbon window and sail vault. But as well as being related linguistically and conceptually,

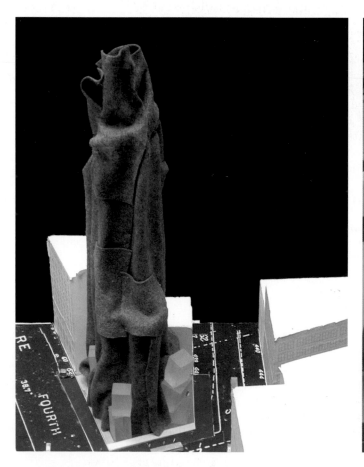

Frank Gehry, Astor Place Hotel, Manhattan, New York (1998) and Lewis Residence (1995)
Though unrealised, the physical models of the tower of the Astor Place Hotel in Manhattan (made using panels of felt) and the Lewis Residence (the central red volume is made with a stiffened velvet) prefigure the dynamic and seemingly casual forms of Gehry's later built works, such as the Guggenheim Museum in Bilbao and the Disney Concert Hall in Los Angeles.

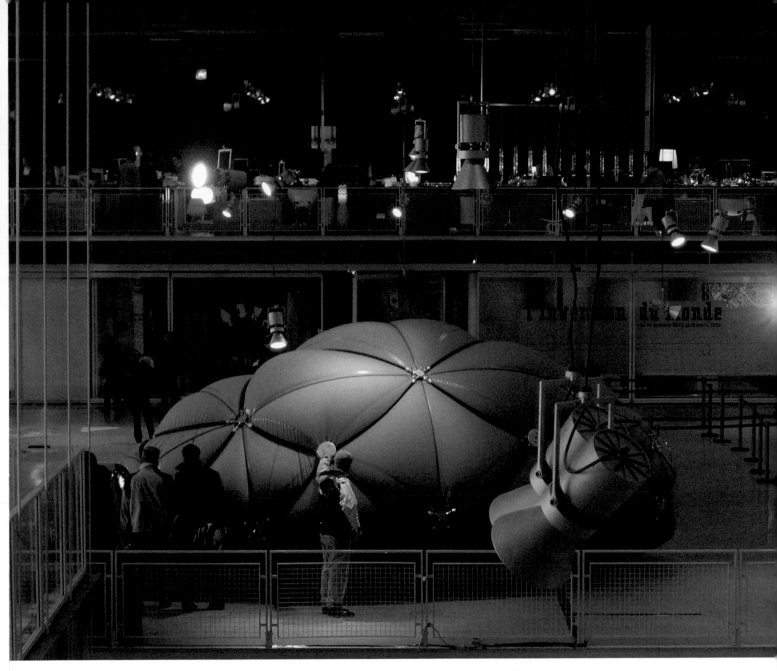

ONL, NSA Muscle installation, 'Non-Standard Architecture' exhibition, Pompidou Centre, Paris, 2003
The NSA Muscle is a pressurised, soft volume wrapped in a mesh of tensile Festo muscles that can change their own length. Orchestrated motions of the individual muscles change the length, height, width and, thus, the overall shape of the Muscle prototype by varying the pressure pumped into the 94 swarming muscles. The balanced pressure–tension combination bends and tapers in all directions.

architecture and textiles are also linked via research programmes. A hybrid of 'architectures' and 'textiles', the word 'architextiles' refers to this body of projects and the ways of thinking and making that join the two.

This hybrid body of work is structured by two linked and converging flows of ideas, two processes of interdisciplinary transmutation that are occurring within and through the meshing of the two disciplines. The increasing 'architecturalisation' of textiles and the increasing 'textilisation' of architecture are, more simply, architectural ways of thinking and doing in textile design, and a textile way of thinking and doing architecture.

Overall, this issue of *AD* uses a broad definition of 'textiles' and therefore brings nonwovens, membranes, meshes, agglomerations of fibres, fabric composites and other hybrids within the scope of its interest, stretching the notion of a fabric/textile and helping to open up existing and new territories of research. It also expands the scope and possibilities for design and encourages a more exhaustive and rigorous challenging of the conventional categories and concepts of both architecture and textiles.

On the surface, there are clear and important commonalities and differences between architecture and textiles – as practices, products, forms of materiality and as innovation. Previously only of specialist and peripheral interest, the significance of tension-based architecture is now on a par with compression structures. The more flexible skeletons and structural envelopes of buildings such as Foster's St Mary Axe and Koolhaas's Seattle Public Library are among the most advanced versions of these new, more tension-based giant textile buildings. For Beasley, such 'evolving structures have steadily increased the role of tension forces, replacing the dense masses of compression-based structures of traditional buildings with open, more efficient systems.'[7]

These types of construction systems are particularly effective in extreme physical conditions, being able to withstand dynamic loading forces that can result in twisting, torsion, buckling and bending, such as encountered during earthquakes, wind-directed heavy snow and during hurricanes. When constructed from lightweight glass and carbon fibres, especially in composites, the textiles are also faster, easier and cheaper to transport, making the construction process simpler and more efficient.

Sociocultural and Economic Drivers of Architextiles
Changes in economics, society and culture have also contributed to the demand for architextiles. In parts of cities such as Tokyo and LA where buildings are constructed and demolished rapidly, architecture begins to take on a nomadic status. The shifting sites of architectural programmes in the accelerating cycles of economic global and sociocultural capitalist production systems leads architects and theorists like Herzog & de Meuron, Hani Rashid, Rem Koolhaas and other aestheticians of speed to conclude that conventional architecture is too slow to keep up with significant changes in society and culture. For Herzog & de Meuron, fashion presents a compelling condition for architecture because 'in the world of fashion … things move faster than in architecture – getting dressed, getting undressed, transforming oneself, giving shape, trying out new sculptural possibilities, examining the quality of surface texture, inventing a new style, and discarding it again.'[8]

For architecture to be able, then, to more effectively express and assimilate the accelerating changes in lifestyle, identity and economics that the contemporary globalised world demands, faster *modus operandi*, more like those deployed in fashion and textiles, are necessary. While the computer and its related technologies have compressed the time of the standard architectural production cycle, and while architecture, as designs (disseminated through photography, magazines, new media, films, exhibitions, drawings and models) is able to match the speed of other design disciplines, the realisation and materialisation of built architecture, as yet, cannot.

Architextiles are particularly well suited for temporary, transportable and ephemeral structures. Such structures are propelled by the emergence of new building typologies, programmes and functions as well as by the need to produce architectural solutions able to handle today's larger and more intricate process-based functions and programmes. Economic and faster design-cycle pressures impose these new conditions and situations on architecture and are now fuelling a burgeoning desire for a faster, lighter, smarter, more transportable, easily de/reconstructed and technologically facilitated architecture. New retail, media, cultural, entertainment, leisure and sports events impose new architectural problems to solve in servicing and housing new programmes, functions and phenomena. They demand a more fluid, adaptable, interactive, variable, multimedia functional and dynamic architecture, driving the search for new architextile forms and aesthetics. Architextiles and their paradigmatic affiliations to fashion and textiles now suggest a tantalising, though not unproblematic, set of possible solutions to such new types and scales of architectural problems.

Each of the contributions to this issue of *AD*[9] has been selected to highlight a unique yet distinct perspective, and together they offer a new and representative view on the

Judit Kimpian, 'Pneumatrix', RCA Department of Architecture, London, 2001
The 13-metre (43-foot) deployable and flexible theatre for up to 1,000 people was developed after research with leading manufacturers and research centres in Germany, France and the Netherlands. Constructed using automated fabrication systems, such as computer-driven weaving, coating, cutting and welding, it features a soft rib structure that defines the enclosure and can be reconfigured through the dynamic shape change occurring in the flexible 'smart' webs that span between the ribs and work as dynamic actuators.

ONL, Textile Growth Monument, Tilburg Textile Museum, the Netherlands, 2005
ONL has here taken the image of the *herdgangen* (community) as the structuring substance for the imagined network of steel beams. The image combines the growth of Tilburg with the flourishing aspect of Tilburg as a textile city. During the night the movements of the public activate sensors that control LEDs in the open ends of the connected steel beams. Moving through and around the monument, visitors thus create their own choreography of light.

significant topics, projects, people, rigour and imagination involved in the innovative meshworking of architecture and textiles. The issue does not privilege built over unbuilt work or any particular style, aesthetic or architectural position. Rather its aim is to find as many ways as possible to probe the field and begin to stretch and test its limits. The historical threads, the academic and professional contributions, as well as the futurological, utopian and the more fantastical speculations shot through these provide alternative scopes of thought. As a whole, it attempts to demonstrate that textiles present an increasingly fascinating and invaluable resource for architecture as well as for our complicating cities and for the humanity they are spinning into the future. ∆

Notes
1. S Hanna and PA Beasley, 'A transformed architecture', in M McQuaid (ed), *Extreme Textiles*, Thames & Hudson (London), 2005, pp 103–4.
2. KW Forster, 'Pieces for four and more hands', in P Ursprung (ed), *Herzog & de Meuron: Natural History*, Lars Muller and Canadian Centre for Architecture (Baden), 2002, p 51. Archaeologists date the first permanent construction and the earliest evidence of constructed textiles to approximately after the last Ice Age, around 7,000 years ago, and believe the first building materials were textiles based on the form of wattle-and-thatch construction, not on a compression-based masonry form.
3. No distinction is made here between the four major spatial design disciplines of interior design, architecture, urban design and landscape design. For brevity they are all referred to as 'architecture'.
4. Bradley Quinn, *The Fashion of Architecture*, Berg Publishers (Oxford), 2003.
5. Sarah Braddock Clarke and Marie O'Mahony, *Techno Textiles: Revolutionary Fabrics for Fashion and Design No 2*, Thames & Hudson (London), 2005.
6. Such as Deleuze's 'fold', Hani Rashid's 'fluid architectures', Kaas Oosterhuis's 'hyperbody' and 'e-motive' architecture, Marcos Novak's 'liquid architecture' and related 'hyper-architectures' and 'trans-architectures'.
7. Hanna and Beasley, op cit.
8. *Natural History*, op cit, p 26.
9. This issue was made possible only with support from Jose and Charo Garcia, Nigel Coates, Fenella Collingridge, Jonathan Goslan, Christopher Frayling, Clare Johnston, Jane Rendell and the participants in this project from the RCA, Bartlett and the AA. Thanks also to Anne Toomey for collaborating extensively with me on this subject, and to Helen Castle and *AD* for commissioning and creating this issue with me.

Prologue for a History and Theory of Architextiles

Mark Garcia substantiates the place of architextiles in architectural design and theory by tracing its history, its primacy in the present and its future potential. It is an overview that takes in Ottoman palaces, Frederick Schinkel, Gottfried Semper, Mies van der Rohe, and a new generation of contemporary grand-scale structures, as well as the visionary.

I believe there is box-thought, the thought we call rigorous, like rigid, inflexible boxes and sack-thought, like systems of fabrics. Our philosophy lacks a good organum of fabrics; I often dream of it. If we had one, many tricks would no longer be possible, but reason would be spared much inflexibility ... Elasticity is not always a sin against straightforward reason ... Let us learn to negotiate soft logics ... Let us finally laugh about those who called rigorous what was precisely their soft discourse. And let us no longer scorn what is soft – fluid ensembles.
Michel Serres[1]

Architecture's relationship with textiles has traditionally been of peripheral interest in the central theories of architecture. This inattention to what is a critical conceptual and material dimension in Islamic, Asian, African, tensile, mobile, pneumatic and vernacular branches of architecture has not troubled many critics. It is therefore timely that this neglect of textiles in architecture is now in reversal. Architects, theorists, engineers and designers are now making bold claims for the importance of this disciplinary confluence and its increasing centrality in architecture. Textiles now offer a significant, unique and expanding range of possibilities for innovation. The historical, theoretical, visual and built evidence of the ways in which textiles and textile concepts can be used and realised in architecture conclusively supports such a claim. The evidence also suggests that the architecture–textiles relationship provides both a unique and illuminating account of the present state and possible futures of architecture and of the city.

The analysis begins in the 15th century, when the relationship between architecture and textiles (though prehistoric) began to change rapidly and in more innovative ways. Tracing the genealogy of this relationship, through a chronological survey of designs and theory, to the present period, it describes and explains some of the key points of intersection within the two disciplines, and ends by synthesising the surveyed set of precedents into a group of abstract concepts and qualities that together suggest the possibility for a coherent theorisation of architextiles. How this link might develop in the future is suggested in a number of speculative and experimental projects.

This survey considers the architecture–textiles relationship across four of its most frequently occurring forms: when a textile or textile-based process is used as a metaphor, when a textile-like spatial structure (such as a weave) is produced in architecture, when textiles (or textile composites) are used as a real material in a real building, and where textiles appear in architectural theory and texts.

Early Architextiles

For centuries, the qualities and properties of textiles as a material group were largely excluded from most architecture theory and from architectural production itself. Textiles and their qualities and properties were kept firmly indoors, within interiors. Until the advent of high-performance and technical textiles in the 20th century, this material group was perceived as temporary, incendiary, fragile, unstable, high maintenance and low performance. Though the technologies for tensile structures and metal meshes were available in the ancient world, they were, in general, conspicuously unexploited in architecture. Fashion and textiles were also traditionally associated with crafts, the feminine, frivolity, the ephemeral and the sensuous and, as such, trivialised in mainstream

14th-century ceramic detail from the Nazrid Palace of the Alhambra in Granada. A product of the mathematical geometry of the late Nazrid dynasty, the knotted, interlaced patterns in the solid ceramics and architecture of the Alhambra are derived from the aesthetics and design and production processes of Islamic textiles.

Painting in the collection of the Musée Carnavalet in Paris by JG Soufflot of the ceremony of the laying of the first stone of the new church of St Geneviève, Paris, 1764. Few of these 1:1 textile architectural models have survived.

Stefanie Surjo, Bio-Tissue Hotel, 2005.

architecture. The tacit, physical and object-embodied materials knowledge of tent makers, tailors, couturiers, weavers, sail makers and textile designers, for example, meant that such vocations were viewed as more 'manual' and prosaic pursuits in comparison to the more 'intellectual' disciplines of art and design (such as engineering, sculpture and architecture).

Many of the historical examples of textile-based architecture have perished due to the lack of durability of the materials used; and because the efforts of the makers and designers within this field were not thought worthy of recording, preserving or of scholarship, most of our early knowledge of these practices remains patchy. While textiles produced for interiors have survived in better condition, few early tensile and ephemeral textile architectures can still be found today. Aside from the almost ubiquitous textile structures of nomadic societies, notable examples include the great awnings of the Colosseum in Rome, the gigantic tent palaces of the Mongol emperors of China, the Ziggurat Aqur Quf near Baghdad (c 1400 BC) and the 'Field of the Cloth of Gold' event held in 1520.[2]

15th- to 19th-century Architextiles
Early textile-based architectures can also be found in less temporary forms than traditional solid and compression-based structures. The Ottoman Palace of Topkapi Sarayi,[3] Istanbul, was erected on the convenient site of the sultan's former military encampment, on the summit of the main hill of Sultanahmet. As architectural historians have demonstrated, the plan, tensile-tectonics and morphology of the palace are derived from the forms, plans, meanings and circulation and access protocols of the earlier Ottoman tent

encampments.[4] The interiors, and some of the structural and tectonic components (as with the 13th- and 14th-century Nazrid palaces of the Alhambra in Granada, Spain, and the mobile tent-palaces of the Mughal emperors in India), are directly derived from the textile geometries, patterns and structural properties of the knots, carpets and wall hangings of their earlier, less permanent tent-like structures.

The gradual move away from textiles to solid versions of the same buildings continued throughout the 17th and 18th centuries and entered mainstream architectural practice in western Europe via the modelling process. The obsession during this period with the mimesis of movement led to the permanent giant stone-textiles of the baroque and the rococo and thus textiles began to re-enter the architectural modelling and design process in more explicit ways. Textile models and full-scale prototypes of commissioned buildings were occasionally erected as part of the design development, and were spectacles in themselves. For example, a painting by PA Demachy commemorates the occasion (in 1764) of the completion of a full-scale, *in situ* canvas replica of Jacques-Germain Soufflot's church of St Geneviève in Paris.

19th-Century Architextiles and Gottfried Semper
The 18th and 19th centuries included brief periods when high-profile interiors that drew on tent aesthetics emerged in rooms for Friedrich Wilhelm II's Marble Palace (1790), for Napoleon at Malmaison, and at the Charlottenhof Palace, Potsdam, by Schinkel.[5] Throughout the 19th century, the key technical architectural innovations that architecture drew from textiles continued to be in terms of the tensile-based, networked grid and steel meshes and other structures that were developed for industrial and civil engineering projects.

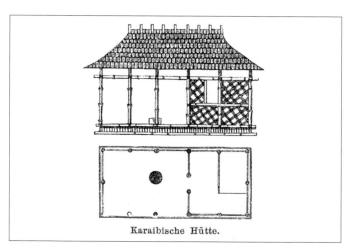

Karaibische Hütte.

Drawing of a Caribbean hut from Semper's *Der Stil in den technischen und tektonischen Künsten oder prakitsche Ästhetik*, Vol 1, 1878. Semper's theory of the 'four elements of architecture' came to him after a visit to a similar hut that was part of the Great Exhibition of 1851. He dissected the hut into four 'essential' and discrete parts (foundations, frame, hearth and fabric walls). This formulation of his 'four elements' of architecture has been interpreted by later, modern theorists and designers as an important, textile-based reconceptualisation of architecture.

Frei Otto, Suspended City, 1960
A simple but original drawing, this image is a rare and imaginative translation of Otto's early tensile architectures and their conical forms into a new type of design for a future city.

The thinking of the Enlightenment, Rationalism and the Industrial Revolution periods began to probe into the inherent abstract qualities of the diagram of the textile. In the Deleuzian sense of the diagram as an 'abstract machine', the diagram of the textile as a networked, woven and flexible mesh began to emerge as a conceptual tool in the thinking of Gottfried Semper (1803–79).

The son of a north German wool-factory owner, Semper became an architect, theorist and, later, the founding professor of architecture at the ETH Zurich. After studying Assyrian textiles in the Louvre, he came to London where he was struck both by Paxton's Crystal Palace[6] and an exhibit of a 'primitive' hut within it. In his treatise *The Four Elements of Architecture* (1851), Semper redefined the wall as a spatial enclosure, or '*wand*', rather than as a structural and critical tectonic member ('*mauer*'). He referred to a building's envelope as an example of 'clothing' and found a common etymological root to the German words for 'dress' and 'wall'. Likening textiles to built surfaces he described both as types of 'veiling'. For him it was the hanging wall-carpets and their status as nonstructural spatial dividers that made them 'the true walls, the visible boundaries of space'.[7]

Also, for Semper the knot is etymologically related to the seam, which is based on the idea of the continuity of bands and threads at joining points. He describes the knot as the oldest tectonic joint in history and supports this claim with the evidence that in German the words 'joint' and 'knot' share a similar linguistic root.[8] Semper's new notions of a textile-based architecture represented a distinct break with previous theories of architecture and influenced later 20th-century Postmodern theories of space.

20th-Century and Modern Architextiles

French, German and American Modernism contributed greatly to the development of the nexus of architecture and textiles. Both Mies van der Rohe and Frank Lloyd Wright used textiles at certain points in their careers. In 1912, Mies, like Soufflot before him, used a full-scale *in situ* canvas model during the design development for the Kröller-Müller House in Wassenaar, the Netherlands, and Wright's Ennis-Brown House (1923) in LA was the result of research into developing what he referred to as 'textile blocks', large panels and walls constructed from concrete and cement blocks, moulded into the forms of his complex geometric designs and linked together with a lattice of metal rods. Made with little quality control, these are now deteriorating rapidly.

During the 1910s and 1920s, the idea of urban structural networks and a more densely interconnected, multilevel morphology of the city, more akin to the diagram of a textile, began to appear in a number of utopian drawings and designs for the future city. In 1908, Moses King's 'Cosmopolis of the Future' and William Leigh's 'Visionary City', published in *Cosmopolitan* magazine, both presented designs of a Manhattan-like city, connected across each level with bridge-like linking structures holding double-decker railroads and

The giant architextiles of Manhattan's advertising architecture are proliferating across the city and increasing in scale. A materialisation and mutation of 'supergraphics', they are designed without architects.

streets in the sky. In 1913, Harvey W Corbett published a similar, more detailed version of the same concept in *Scientific American*. For Futurist architects like Sant'Elia in his 1914 'Manifesto of Futurist Architecture', textiles were part of the new range of materials that should be used in architecture because of their ability to deliver 'the maximum of elasticity and lightness'.[9] In 1937, Le Corbusier unveiled his tensile Pavilion des Temps Nouveaux at the Paris World Fair, but it was only later in the century that ideas such as these began to be translated into serious proposals for urban, megastructural, tensile-based networked cities like that envisioned by Paul Maymont in his Ville Flottante of 1959.

Parallel research into pneumatic structures continued throughout the century, leading to the development of airships, hovercraft and large-scale complex pneumatic structures such as Grimshaw's Eden Project in Cornwall (2002). In 1947 and 1948, Buckminster Fuller developed the concept of 'structural synergy', where the nature of the structural system is contingent on the behaviour of the parts taken as a whole system. It was during this period of experimentation with early tensegrity systems that Fuller developed the concept of textiles as exemplary adaptable and flexible systems for architecture. In the 1960s, Frei Otto's Suspended City and Fuller's 1964 new Harlem projects (New York) applied these same ideas to their curving, tensile-based, networked, multilevel city designs. Throughout the decade, Otto continued to explore the structural properties of minimal surfaces through the use of simple wool-thread 'machines' with which he began generating nonlinear structural surfaces and optimised architectural networks and forms.[10]

Postmodern Architextiles

For writers like Sean Hanna and Phillip Beasley it was the more complex textile-like structures of the steel meshes of the Eiffel Tower in Paris and those inside Eiffel and Bartholdi's Statue of Liberty of 1886 that were seen as the 19th-century precursors of the architectural macrotextiles of the 20th and 21st centuries. Hanna and Beasley argue that 'a new generation of giant-scale textiles is at the core of a revolution in architecture'[11] and cite Foster's St Mary Axe in London, the OMA Seattle Public Library and Testa & Weiser's Carbon Tower as the exemplars of this new movement.

Only with the advent of the computer and the digital meshes of building skins and NURBS surfaces did architecture begin to take on more of the qualities of textiles in the 1990s. The modelling and building of such architectural megatextiles and the translation of physical textiles and textile techniques into architecture with the aid of the computer has been a sustained preoccupation for architectural theorists and advanced research architects like Lars Spuybroek, for whom Semper and Otto have been formative precedents. From 1998, many of Spuybroek's projects have dealt specifically with the textile tectonics of complex buildings and propose radical new urban concepts, such as the ParisBrain (2001). These draw directly, explicitly and extensively on design methodologies-driven textile tectonics. Though, like Alsop and Perrault, Spuybroek's work represents the cutting edge of architextiles, his rigorous and intense research in this field is the single but spectacular example of its type.

Today, Zaha Hadid's work is presented by her office under the categories 'ribbons' and 'carpets,'[12] and Dominique Perrault and Will Alsop both have strong bodies of prize-winning international projects behind them which, like the work of a rising number of international and emerging architects (many included in this issue of *AD*) have been explicitly driven by research on architectural textiles and textile architectures. The integration of architectural textiles with new technologies has also been the preserve of respected academic research institutes.[13] A number of the most imaginative and innovative interactive architecture projects, for example Diller + Scofidio's Brain Coat (2002) for their artificial Cloud 'Blur' in Switzerland, Enric Ruiz Geli's Hotel Habitat (2006) and ONL's kinetic-architectural experiments such as 'Muscle Body' (2005) and the Textile Growth Monument in Tilburg (2005) have all synthesised interactive technologies and textile methods of designing to create dynamic, narrative and kinetic qualities in architecture.

Theoretical Adjacencies and Precursors of Architextiles

As textiles and their fashion-related aspects enjoyed an increased prominence in architecture, their links to related disciplines at a theoretical level have also (since Gilles Deleuze's work on the 'fold') begun to spread and strengthen. For other Postmodern theorists like Jacques Derrida, 2.5-D architecture theorists and landscape urbanists, it is other, more specific qualities shared between architecture and textiles that are of interest. For Derrida it was Bernard

Future Systems, Magasins Generaux, Paris, 2004
The integration of disparate programmes, existing structures and new architectural elements with a single form draped over the whole creates a 'mountain' in the centre of Paris. Projects like this (reminiscent of the many projects by the artist Christo) use textile-like forms to create landform structures that blur the boundaries between landscape, architecture and textile.

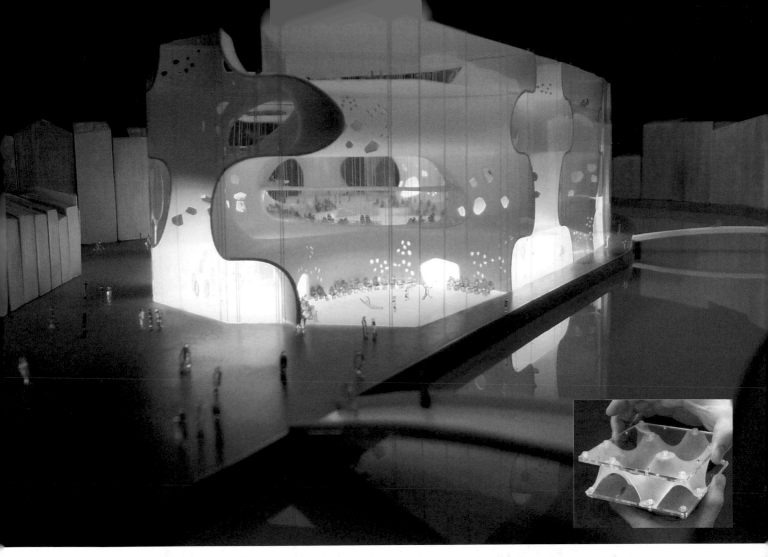

Toyo Ito and Andrea Branzi, Forum for Music, Dance and Visual Culture, Ghent, Belgium, 2004
The result of using the tensile membrane conceptual model, the continuous sinusoidal floor plates and their expression onto and around the entire facade generates a smooth and seamless 360-degree kinetic flow of space, light and depth throughout the entire building. Inset: A continuous single membrane stretched and pinned between Perspex sheets was used as the conceptual model to generate the topography and aesthetics of interior and exterior, horizontal and vertical, in a simple fabric operation.

Tschumi and his use of the grid and cross-programming (for example in his project for the Parc de la Villette) that was the most textile-like in architecture.[14] According to Derrida, the text is a textile, a veil,[15] a texture, as both a network of abstract and porous referents and meanings and as a decentred, fabricated surface. The question of meaning is a necessary one. If for Derrida 'architecture must have meaning', then the question of architecture's links to textiles becomes urgent when considering the wider social and cultural context of this disciplinary twinning. Questions of architecture's problematic relations to fashion, advertising and media, and its role in societies and cities networked into the accelerating systems of globalised capitalist production and consumption, are important ones. The giant building-scale textiles such as can be found in today's Manhattan, and the new media-driven giant screens of tomorrow's hyper- and media-architectures, are forcing this issue and proposing problematic solutions.

The importance of the theorisation of field-effect architecture and field-spaces,[16] and of new architectural building skins (such as the '2.5 dimensional' in architecture),[17] is also stimulating the interfacing of architecture with textiles. On a larger scale, the concepts being developed in landscape urbanism theories of spatial design[18] share common concepts and qualities with today's textile design research. Of central interest in both of these areas are the problems of structuring, deforming and informing continuous, convoluted, flexible, polycentric and multiscale surfaces with unpredictable, multidimensional and broad ranges of factors.

Certain new Postmodern architecture theories developed after Deleuze's text on the 'fold'[19] are articulating a new metaphysical and ontological characterisation of space. These new theories are concerned with the dynamic, interactive, multimedia, flexible, ephemeral, event- and process-based methods of designing and experiencing space. Opposed to

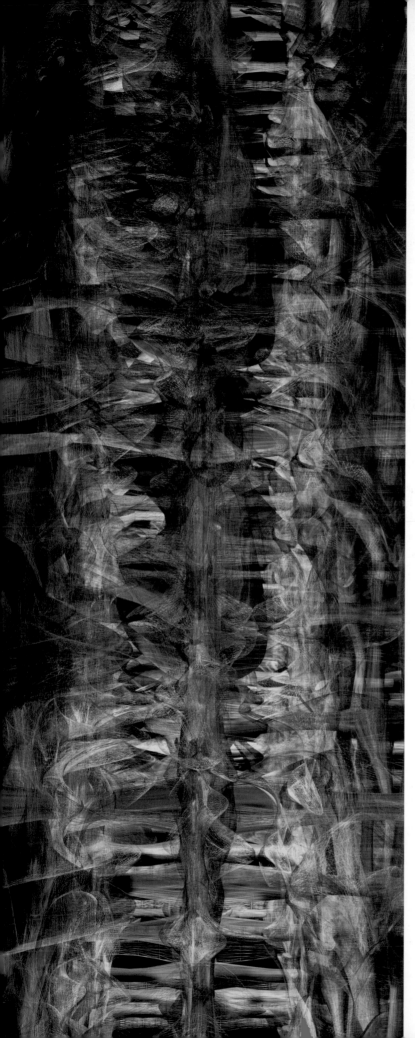

historical paradigms based on the Vitruvian concept of *firmitas* and the conception of architectural space as permanent, finished, durable, static, hard and compression-based, they articulate a new space – one that is never finished, never static, in a continuous state of provisional and transitional becoming. They describe this paradigm as a literal reorientation of architecture from the solid to the liquid and gaseous states of matter. A transition stage from the solid to the liquid, the material qualities and concepts of textiles and textile design, makes them particularly relevant to this new paradigm of spatial design.

Towards a New Theorisation of Architextiles

The manifold ways of theorising or materialising collisions between textiles and architecture and the possible transferable qualities and effects of each for the other can now be argued to be of central importance to architecture per se. Moving towards any useful theorisation of this ragbag of historical precedents and concepts requires a synthesis of the salient textile qualities and concepts that have been embodied in the architectural projects and texts in this issue, and in general. The qualities and concepts, as described in this body of work, are often contradictory, vague, but approximate. Together they reflect some of the paradoxical but real qualities and concepts in many of the most interesting new (and older) textiles and buildings today. Grouped and considered as a whole, such qualities and concepts seem to offer a robustly useful framework for understanding, interpreting and designing contemporary architecture. Moreover, these categories and qualities suggest further, as yet unexploited, programmes for their materialisation and realisation in both architecture and textiles: soft, flexible, convoluted, networked, continuous, dynamic, variable, woven, latticed, folded, adaptable, translucent, tensile, pneumatic, pleated, creased, knotted, pliable, porous, veiled, elastic, plastic, supple, knitted, draped, flowing, interactive, patterned, comforting, cosy, fashionable, enveloping, clothing, protecting, lighter, faster, stronger and smarter.

The Future of Architextiles

Utopian and futuristic representations of the architecture–textile nexus are also of interest for the designers and researchers of today, and those of the future. They raise aesthetic, social and cultural issues that provoke more complex, sophisticated critiques and discourses within architecture, unencumbered by the problematic needs of clients and material and financial constraints. Speculative, conceptual and fictional architextiles provide useful counterfactual thought-experiments on subjects as diverse as

Stefanie Surjo, Bio-Tissue Hotel, 2005
CAD models of a section of the skin for the facade development of the Bio-Tissue Hotel (UCL diploma final-year project) investigating the networks of connective tissues, spatial forms and aesthetics of biological architectural skins.

Signalpain, Expo 2002, Yverdon, Switzerland
The woven Corten-steel strips of the interior, dense with hanging textile and foam threads, provide the sensation of inhabiting a loosely woven textile.

dynamically reconfigurable cities and landscapes, nanotechnologies, smart materials, carbon-based architectures and biotechnological buildings. Innovative and high-tech textiles and giant meshes are now being proposed by ambitious projects like ETALAB's Tate in Space, Testa & Weiser's Carbon Tower and the giant megastructure of the Shimizu Corporation Mega-City Pyramid project.[20]

In nature, there are four main biological, low-density, fibre-based structures: cellulose in plants, chitin in insects and crustaceans, collagen in animals and silk in arachnids. These structures are interesting to biomimetics researchers as they are able to vary their form and density, allowing them to perform a variety of different functions. Complex functions and qualities like self-repair, growth and replication are the organic qualities of architecture being sought after within this model of research currently shared by architects, textile designers, engineers and other scientists. Provocative projects like Stefanie Surjo's Bio-Tissue Hotel examine the aesthetic possibilities of biotextiles in architecture. Surjo's study and conceptual drawings of the connective-tissue type of space is an upgraded version of the networked forms of the future city presented in the early 1900s by King, Leigh and Corbett, and is a convincing and haunting anticipation of the possible and visceral bio-architextile city of the future.

The historical and hypothetical projects and great temporary textile cities that have emerged throughout history[21] share their textile qualities and concepts with the more permanent, avant-garde designs of many of today's more innovative architecture. It is such significant and original contributions to the theory, history and practice of architecture that insist that a close and rigorous relationship of architecture to textiles will be of continuing value in the future.

Signalpain, Expo 2002, Yverdon, Switzerland
The woven Corten-steel strips of the four facades of this pavilion building, as well as its interior, dense with hanging textile and foam threads, provide the sensation of inhabiting a loosely woven textile.

Notes

1. M Serres and B Latour, 'In the city: agitated multiplicity', *Conversations on Science, Culture and Time*, University of Michigan Press, 1995, p 15.
2. The event consisted of the creation of a temporary city made of tents/textiles. The most ornate buildings were made of a cloth of gold, hence the name. The event was commemorated in a large painting by Holbein the Elder as well as the various prints derived directly from this work.
3. The palace of the Ottoman sultan and seat of the imperial government from the 15th to the 18th century.
4. See Gulru Necipoglu, *Architecture, Ceremonial, and Power: The Topkapi Palace in the Fifteenth and Sixteenth Centuries*, MIT Press (Cambridge, MA), 1992.
5. KM Koch, *Membrane Structures*, Prestel (Germany), 2004, p 26.
6. In a 1852 speech, Joseph Paxton explained the structural principle behind his Crystal Palace as consisting of an iron structural frame acting like a 'table' and the enclosing glass envelope as a 'tablecloth'. See W Herrmann, *Gottfried Semper: In Search of Architecture*, MIT Press (Cambridge, MA), 1984.
7. G Semper (1851), *The Four Elements of Architecture and Other Writings*, trans H Malgrave and M Herman, Cambridge University Press, 1989.
8. Knot theory, though a relatively new branch of mathematics, is now finding applications in biology, chemistry, materials science and physics. Projects such as Objectile's Semper Pavilion (1997), ARM's knotted roof for a part of the National Museum of Australia (2001), projects by Arup's Advanced Geometry Unit, NOX, and the Y-Knot forms by Garcia and Goslan (2006) all use ideas from knot topology to generate architectures.
9. M Drudi Gambilo and T Fiori (eds), *Archivi del futurismo*, Deluca (Rome), 1958–62.
10. This work was published, together with Rudolf Trostel, as 'Tensile Structures' in 1967.
11. S Hanna and PA Beasley, 'Transformed architecture in extreme textiles', in M McQuaid (ed), *Extreme Textiles: Designing for High Performance*, Thames & Hudson (London), 2005, p 103.
12. P Schumacher and GF Giusti, *Zaha Hadid Complete Works*, Thames & Hudson (London), 2004.
13. Centres like the Fraunhofer and the ZKM Centre for Art and Media in Karlsruhe, and the Centre for Interactive Cinema Research at the University of New South Wales in Australia, have developed architectural textiles as components of interactive and information-architecture projects.
14. J Derrida, 'Point de folie: Maintenant l'architecture' in B Tschumi, *La Case Vide: La Villette*, Architectural Association (London), 1986.
15. J Derrida, *Dissemination*, Continuum (Athlone), 1981, p 240.
16. For example, S Kwinter, 'La Città Nuova: Modernity and Continuity', in M Hays (ed), *Architecture Theory Since 1968*, Columbia Books of Architecture and MIT Press (London and Cambridge, MA), 2000.
17. T Igarashi, 'Superflat architecture and Japanese subculture', in M Kira and M Terada (eds), *Japan: Towards Totalscape*, NAI (Rotterdam), 2001.
18. Such as James Corner, Florian Biegel, Philip Christou and Ciro Naije, in J Corner, 'Landscape urbanism', in M Mostafavi et al (eds), *Landscape Urbanism: A Manual for the Machinic Landscape*, AA Publications (London), 2003.
19. G Deleuze, *The Fold: Leibniz and the Baroque*, University of Minnesota Press, 1992.
20. MVRDV, *KM3: Excursions on Capacities*, Actar (Barcelona), 2006.
21. Such as the great religious festivals of the Hajj or the Kumb Melas, or during the recovery of cities after disasters such as the San Francisco earthquake of 1906 or the famines, hurricanes and great fires of previous centuries. ⌂

National Museum of Textile Costume, Doha, Qatar

Ushida Findlay Architects

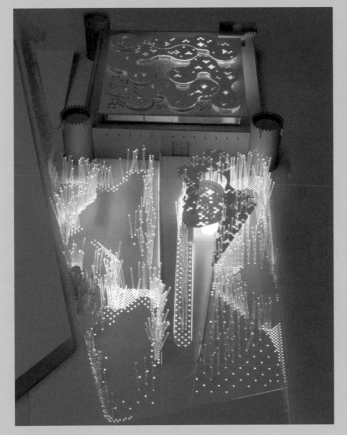

The museum was designed in 2003–04 to embody the subject it is intended to house, namely the fabric, textiles and flowing costumes of the Gulf region. The building is an extension to an existing fort in Doha, the country's capital, and occupies a central courtyard and an extensive excavation below.

The concept used the idea of a solid skein of threads, rather like a brush head. The notional 'threads' thickened to become the columns or vertical service ducts of the building, or delicate screens of the exhibitions, and the dense forest of threads was then carved out to create the exhibition spaces – a weaving of ground into figure. Metal chain-mail mesh walls and thin wire meshes surface and screen interiors and exteriors throughout. Each thread creates a dot point pattern in plan, and the logic behind the resultant Islamic textile-based geometry informed design development. Specifically, as each dot point projected a radius, which described a circle and a matrix of touching and interlocking circles, the circles formed roof, ceiling and floor patterns.

The upper-level space within the courtyard is roofed over to house a café. Its lace-patterned roof of water-cooled concrete allows light to penetrate, but also shields against intense solar gain. The grain is loose and porous, enabling the beautiful light of the region to flood in. This craftfully lit environment would enable Qataris to enjoy the focus of their national costumes in use.

As visitors decend into the exhibition spaces below, the patterning grain of the space becomes finer and the space darker, the focus shifting to become the rich and intense beauty of the inner layers of Arabic dress on display. And in the cool of the evening, a public square above the main body of the museum is animated by a grid of vertical water-jets and light stands, creating an association with the patterns of the local costumes in the museum below. ∆

Kathryn Findlay

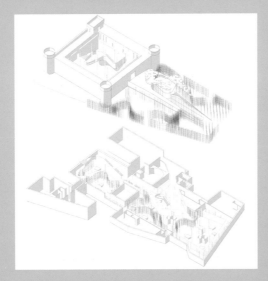

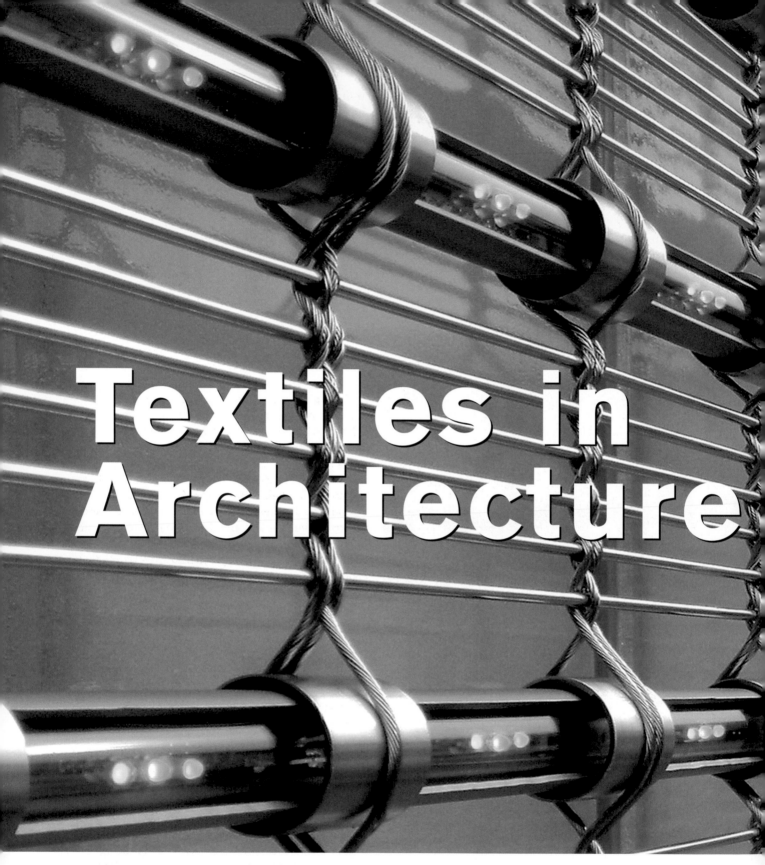

Textiles in Architecture

'The cutting edge in architecture is not sharp, but sensuous and soft.' As textiles begin to emerge as megamaterials, **Bradley Quinn** explains how architects are pioneering new possibilities for soft structures. Fabric-formed environments are fashioning tensile buildings and inflatable pavilions, while the tailoring techniques of braiding, weaving and pleating are building supple skyscrapers and bioclimatic enclosures.

GKD Metal Fabrics, Mediamesh stainless-steel textile
Mediamesh interweaves digital imagery and special LED strips at regular intervals. The LEDs display digital images such as logos, advertising promotions, animation and film, and can be controlled remotely through a Web-based user interface and also interact spontaneously with weather changes.

At first, building with textiles seems riddled with problems – fabrics are usually perceived as flammable, vulnerable to water, impermanent and weak. Architecture is equated with density and mass, while textiles have often been limited to lightweight decorative expressions. Few practitioners would guess that textiles have a long history as an architectural material, giving rise to a tradition of portable habitations and porous buildings several thousand years ago. In the context of buildings, fabrics disappeared as wood, stone, metal and glass became the materials of choice, but recent developments in textile technology have revealed their relevance to architecture today. Even though robust architecture and tactile fabrics may seem irreconcilably diverse, there are threads that bind.

Visionaries know that the cutting edge in architecture is not sharp, but sensuous and soft. At a time when architects are pioneering new structural networks, immersive webs, mobile buildings and fluid exchanges, textiles have revealed a surprising history of modularity and multifunctionality, and an essential narrative function. While early textile structures afforded protection from the elements, they also featured symbols and inscriptions that represented a mode of belonging. The ciphers woven into dwellings were also stitched into clothing, identifying whole groups and forging indissoluble links between architecture, individuals and communities. Today, textiles continue to be loaded with signifiers, and their role in apparel makes fabric a familiar second skin. Textiles are more tactile than conventional construction materials, and their colours, textures and finishes imbue them with stylistic references uncharacteristic of building supplies. Transposed into architecture, textiles endow built structures with attachments and meanings that extend far beyond the occupation of territory. Now, for the first time in many years, the significance of the textile in architecture is being rediscovered.

Many of the visual and intellectual principles underpinning fashion are gaining currency among architects. As tailoring techniques find expression in architecture, the resulting focus on fashion tends to eclipse the vital role that textiles play in contemporary architecture. Apparel and architecture rarely come together in structures built for permanent habitation, but converge where they share mutual skills, practices and ideas. Fabric, in the hands of fashion designers, can craft wearable shelters, while the agency of architecture enables textiles to become built structures. Textiles and architecture can truly become one in the built environment, while fashion is inextricably limited by the body's need for egress.

Textiles have emerged as a material that can interface with built structures on many different levels, resulting in a whole new paradigm of lightweight, interwoven architecture. Textile structures weave in and out of public space, popping up in sports arenas, airports, trade shows, urban parks, shopping centres and residential projects. Felted fabrics provide efficient sources of insulation, which architects piece together like the patchwork of a quilt. Some exterior textiles have a capacity for channelling and reflecting natural light that

Lars Spuybroek, Maison Folie, Lille, France, 2004
Textiles have emerged as a material that can sculpt a building's profile into a variety of unexpected shapes. The undulating facade of this building is created by the stainless-steel Escale textile, the interlocking metal components of which appear to have been knitted together.

known today, are widely used in paving projects, as boundaries markers and to sculpt hilly slopes on flat terrain.

Geotextiles demarcate a new way of thinking about the built environment. By taking built surfaces underground, they subvert the verticality of architecture by projecting architectural space far beyond its outer walls. The proportions of architecture are generally considered to be fixed distinctions, but the presence of geotextiles suggests a continuum of structure and space. Just like other construction materials, geotextiles have the potential to create floor, wall and corner conditions. Such conditions expand the dimensions of a built structure and could mean that a building's epicentre is repositioned beyond the perimeter walls. This type of parafunctional[3] site creates powerful event space that brings materials, programme, place, space and landscape together in a seamless gesture.

Historically, theorists such as Semper viewed the surface in terms of its material presence, but geotextiles are remarkably absent from the surfaces they construct. In his analogy of the carpet and the wall, Semper spoke much of the visible boundaries of space.[4] Geotextiles move in a new direction as they chart boundaries that are not visible, moving Semper's 'walls' beyond the building and into the landscape beyond.

The dynamic exchanges taking place between architecture and textiles are creating a new range of possibilities that take both disciplines in exciting new directions. Not only does today's generation of textiles provide new inspiration for architects, it also presents fresh possibilities for urban planners and developers. As buildings, public space and landscapes are reconceived as a single expression, the potential to experience the cityscape as a tactile arena could change our experience of architecture for ever. ∆

Notes
1. Also known as CAST, the Centre for Architectural Structure and Technology operates within the Faculty of Architecture at the University of Manitoba in Canada.
2. See Claude Lèvi-Strauss, *The Savage Mind*, University of Chicago Press (Chicago, IL), 1968.
3. Refers to the sites Nikos Papastergiadis dubs 'parafunctional spaces'. This term refers to urban spaces in which 'creative, informal and unintended uses overtake the officially designated functions'. See Nikos Papastergiadis, 'Traces left in cities', in *Architectural Design: Poetics in Architecture*, April 2002, p 45.
4. Gottfried Semper, 'Style in the technical arts or practical aesthetics', in *The Four Elements of Architecture and Other Writings*, trans Harry Francis Mallgrove and Wolfgang Herman, Cambridge University Press (New York), 1989.

The Straw House and Quilted Office, 9–10 Stock Orchard Street, Islington, London

Sarah Wigglesworth Architects and Jeremy Till

The project at Stock Orchard Street (2001) is perhaps best known for its use of straw bales for the walls of the house. However, it also uses a number of other unconventional materials, some derived from fabrics. In particular, the office (which is attached to the house) has one wall of sandbags, while the rest of it is wrapped in a quilted fabric.

The Sandbag Wall

The wall to the office that overlooks the nearby railway line was inspired by a wartime picture of the Kardomah coffee house during the Blitz, its plate-glass window protected by a wall of sandbags, refined Londoners attempting to maintain some semblance of normality behind this crude architecture. Fifty years on and the techniques for building in sandbags had been lost, thus the technique used here had to be invented from scratch.

The bags are filled with a mixture of sand, cement and lime, and are tied back to a timber frame. Where most walls are designed to shrug off the effects of time, this one encourages time to pass through and thereby modify it. Over the years, the bags will decay and the mixture will harden, so that eventually a rippling wall of concrete will emerge, left with the rough imprint of cloth.

The window surrounds, for which there are few known precedents, are made from railway sleepers found on the site. The wall was termed Flintstone architecture by the builders. The elevation is designed to be seen from a passing train, a glimpse of the random splattering of openings confusing the sense of scale and place, introducing a moment of strangeness as commuters look up from their papers.

The Quilted Wall

The office is usually seen as a place apart from the home and architecturally assumes an identity of decorum and order, in opposition to the supposedly wilful nature of domestic life. The standard garb for offices is thus that of corporate Modernism – shiny, refined facades attempting to look progressive. This aesthetic is also gendered, the 'rational' male associated with the virtues of the efficient office, leaving the scatty female to the uncanny of home.

But at 9 Stock Orchard Street such categorisations and separation are challenged and disturbed. The part of the office that is not made of sandbags is wrapped in cloth, puckered and buttoned like a domestic quilt. It looks fragile, but is designed to last for years, and then it will be unbuttoned and replaced with something quite else – a provisional architecture resisting the demands for eternity and fixity. The cloth is silicone-faced fibreglass, used on North Sea oil rigs for machine covers, which was then quilted with an insulating layer and inner lining by a tarpaulin maker. The builders called it the 'nappy'.

Together with the sandbags, gabions and straw bales, the quilt forms a repertoire of technologies of the everyday, raiding the catalogues of other disciplines for inspiration – a technology transfer that reverses the normal exchange between architecture and high-technology industries and replaces it with methods that are simple and immediate. Δ

Jeremy Till and Sarah Wigglesworth

Impending Landscapes of the Architextile City

An Interview with Dominique Perrault

The qualities of textiles for Dominique
Perrault 'represent a real expansion of the
feeling of architecture'. Through the
application of highly innovative meshes,
Perrault has realised 'synthetic landscapes'
that introduce an entirely new type of
public space. **Mark Garcia** visited Perrault
in his studio in Paris to discuss his work,
his collaborations with manufacturers and
ultimately his vision for applying textiles to
'a more democratic, human and
pleasurable' type of urban space.

Dominique Perrault is famous for his explicit and extensive textile-based architectural and urban designs. For more than 16 years he has been researching the relationship between textiles and architecture as part of his broader project on the contemporary city. He emerged on to the world stage in 1989 with his competition entry for the new Bibliothèque Nationale in Paris, which propelled his work with meshes on to the international scene. Since then he has continued his research into exploring the structural, functional, emotive and atmospheric effects of an architecture of textile-based properties, ideas and qualities. Many of Perrault's new and recent works demonstrate original spatial moves and concerns that have deepened the scope, depth and value of his particular manner of articulating the relationships between architecture and textiles. His aspirations for further work in this territory are plausible and seductive. Together they signal a mature and sophisticated ability to blend a disparity of architectural styles and aesthetics. His works are suggestive of many of the possible futures of architextiles.

Perrault describes his work in evocative and phenomenological terms, referring to fleeting effects and to the 'speed', 'liquidity', 'softness' and other characteristics of textiles in space. He has traced these qualities to his fascination, as a child, for watching boat sails. For Perrault these qualities represent a real expansion of the feeling of architecture. He explains that when beginning work on a building he aims to control and enhance the diversity of functions in one unique envelope:

'I try to connect the complexity and specificity of a box with functions, with the environment. My strategy or concern is how to link the disposition of a volume in space with its context. With installation and conceptual art, the object transforms a space in another space with a precise and specific intervention. I manage the presence of the context around the building, around this box, with another element. This element has become the fabric. With this flexible, supple material, this tissue, it is possible to develop, around a very functional box, a special in-between space that also connects the box to the geography of the site. I have been interested in the Land/Art approach because I am constantly investigating new relationships between architecture and landscape. I like to build landscapes, not just buildings.'

This explicitly 'landscape' mode of practice is not surprising from an architect trained in urbanism. Perrault's forms, he agrees, can be described persuasively not just as textiles, but as synthetic landscapes; mountains, lakes, skies, forests, waterfalls, rivers, volcanoes, clouds and caves. His architectural conceptualisation of nature and landscape is, however, more complex and subtle than a simple

Dominique Perrault, Fondation Pinault, Paris, 2001
Model of the museum interior. Perrault's articulation creates a set of deliberately composed, leftover spaces between the exteriors of the disparate, hard and orthogonal masses of the museum and the soft, flowing, but monumentally unifying surface of the exterior membrane.

Dominique Perrault, Las Teresitas, Tenerife, Spain, 2003
Computer rendering of the mesh and the shaded public spaces it creates beside the pools and gardens facing the lower levels of the mountainous hotel.

Computer rendering. Detail of an opening through the mesh and into the lower level of the beachside resort hotel interior.

Dominique Perrault, Berlin Velodrome and Swimming Pool, Germany, 1999
Aerial photograph of the velodrome and swimming pool. The reflective external meshes of both volumes change continuously in the weather and light. Sunk into landscaping, the buildings can appear as a rippled lake-surface.

iconographic or representational gesture. He believes that 'nature, as a stable category, does not exist. Humans create nature, an artificial nature. During the 18th century we invented the English and French parks; these are not natural, but cultural. We have accepted the situation that the planet has to change in some ways because we have built cities and huge agglomerations. But this is not negative. If we accept this vision, we should control and build a specific nature for people. This is not just architecture or landscape, but both.'

Common to much of Perrault's work is the balanced assimilation and representation of contradictions, variations of control and contrasts of oppositions. Progressive projects have examined a broad range of textile qualities. For example, he describes his past projects as, variously, 'veil', 'evening dress', 'smock', 'vestment', 'slipcover', 'curtain' and 'drape'. His translations of textiles into architecture and urbanism are set to continue and he is clear and confident when talking of his feeling that his imagination will continue to fuel future research in these fields:

'The main statements now are to do with the presence of a space in-between, especially public spaces. The question now is how to introduce public spaces into huge projects. My first experience was with the French Bibliothèque Nationale, which has a huge void, with no walls and no fences around the building. This building is totally open to the district, and I use a void like a material. The strategy with the mesh is to make it possible to create this void space in-between the box and the mesh. The space should be specifically public in status. It should be free, a real urban space.'

The corruption of public space has been of critical concern for architects and urban designers throughout the 1990s. Oldenburg's notion of the 'third place',[1] Wolf Prix's 'free space'[2] and 'blank spaces', and Aaron Betsky's 'making of nothingness'[3] in urban space are all similar strategic responses to this decline in the quality of the public realm. The decline, frequently touted as a crisis in the city, is almost always blamed on the dark underbelly of globalisation and the forces of late turbo-capitalism. Will Alsop, Rem Koolhaas and Wolf Prix have all contributed critical texts and works of architecture in response to this crisis. However, what is peculiar to Perrault's spatial strategies is that, from the Badalona Sports Complex in Spain (1998) to the present day, his responses to the same crisis are frequently textile related and are becoming increasingly innovative in ambition, as well as in their material, technical and structural resolution.

Perrault's Beijing Olympic Swimming pool and Pompidou-Metz projects feature large expanses of empty public space. His tactics in both works aim at developing the practical and artistic consequences of these types of design moves. The excitement, for Perrault, is in the use of the mesh to protect people with architecture and to encourage them to reconsider their use and sense of the city, 'to stop and experience another ambience, another quality. It's neither in nor out, it's more subtle than that. It's an emotional attitude. I think this kind of situation could introduce a new quality into urban

Dominique Perrault, CCTV Building, Beijing, China, 2002
Computer-rendered side elevation. The mesh panels smoothly integrate the vertical L-shape of the main building mass with the horizontal ground plane. Curving in a pixilated waterfall over the corner of the two facades it merges the building with the landscaped main entrance and the plaza in front.

Model of the fine-gauge metal mesh. The forest- and textile-like cliff face of independent mesh-covered panels then hovers out over the main public space.

space. This is becoming more important with the rise of huge buildings, for example in Asia. Asia is demanding megastructures. If you build a huge building, it's not absolutely necessary to build a huge lobby or a huge atrium. But if you wrap this building, you can introduce another quality to the space, a specificity to the space around it, a new type of urban lobby. This is more like a promenade, where urban life is encouraged. I think it could work in many places with local and precise modifications.

'In Naples we are working on a project that is essentially a metal forest. It is not a building, it's more of a sculpture, a canopy to design shadows. Using this approach requires the sensitivity of a fashion designer who tries to create a specific relationship between the identity, body and garment of the person. It's not only about function, it's about adding a twist, an emotive contradiction – more than just functional. I also develop a project slowly, step by step, through designing with the environmental and other aspects of the context and the programme, with precision and specificity. This is about creating an intimate fit between the concept of the building and its context.'

This approach to urbanism and public space could be applied in London where few tactics of this type have ever been attempted. As a spatial catalyst for denser, more complex patterns of urban, cultural and social life, Perrault's designs for the giant textiles he discusses above could also operate effectively in hot cities where the main environmental and climatic problems are solar heat gain and excessive light levels. In his most recent projects Perrault is

moving in a trajectory of increasing scale. Pragmatically, he is critical of the overhyped and impractical aspects of more overtly technical textile innovations, and he notes that 'there are some interesting new technical textiles that have been developed, but they are too smart. They are very expensive and are often like a gadget. They are often too high-tech for certain uses. I would like to design a mesh with integrated solar panels. High-tech solutions are sometimes not necessary. Low-tech solutions are sometimes enough. Developing new textiles is important for architecture, but how existing materials are used is also a huge and exciting area in which to progress.'

A new tendency in Perrault's work that first emerged early in 2006 with his Library and Research Centre in Seville is the introduction of pattern and its local craft origins and meanings to the design of space and place. Perrault's operation within an increasingly wide range of stylistic moves is indicated in this project and its new treatment of computer-designed and generated effects. His research into pattern is directly related to his textile way of architectural thinking and making. As he explains: 'One of the qualities of fabric is the ease with which you can design its pattern. It's one of its basic yet most fascinating qualities. My previous architecture operated with an almost minimalist, pure and geometrical pattern. With fabric, we can create very complex patterns. If you then start designing with light, reflections, shadows and the shimmering presence of tissues, you can begin creating layers of patterns, printed on materials like glass, which can be designed to function like a device, an optical instrument

Dominique Perrault, Beijing Olympic Swimming Pool, China, 2003
External corner view of the new Beijing swimming pool. The two main stacked volumes are each clothed with their own semitransparent fabric covering which tapers out over the main building mass, providing large expanses of overhead enclosure for the surrounding public spaces.

for making new patterns of spatial and perceptual effects.

'The technical and material details and connections required to create these high-quality effects must be to the standard of couture or tailoring. This is significant: the quality of the material is in the detail and the quality of the devices that fix it. If the edge and the materials are perfectly designed, the quality of the overall project and its feeling increases. Textiles change their properties depending on their tension and the detail of their structure. When you install these kinds of textiles, its not ornamentation or decoration, it's not fake – the structures and patterns have real physical and aesthetic qualities. We are working with manufacturers and industrial partners to develop specific devices to fix, connect and begin modifying these textiles in original ways.'

In Perrault's successful collaborations with mesh manufacturers and producers, he has altered the nature of architectural construction and its system of production through his development of new building fabrics with German manufacturer GKD. His work in this field has also helped to revitalise GKD and has opened up new international markets for the architectural meshes, markets recently estimated to be worth approximately 20 million euros annually.[4] For Perrault, 'collaborations of this sort have been exciting because the work is new for everyone.

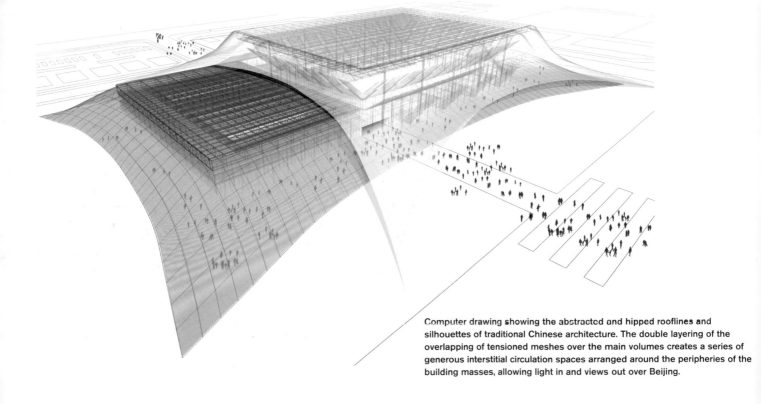

Computer drawing showing the abstracted and hipped rooflines and silhouettes of traditional Chinese architecture. The double layering of the overlapping of tensioned meshes over the main volumes creates a series of generous interstitial circulation spaces arranged around the peripheries of the building masses, allowing light in and views out over Beijing.

Dominique Perrault, Centre Pompidou-Metz, France, 2003
Computer rendering. The external mesh skin also functions as a media surface, suggesting the changing contents and events within the museum.

Collaboration is absolutely necessary. I think we should introduce not only some other attitude and vision, but other cultures. At the moment we are working with a Japanese company on new concepts for meshes. The Japanese have another culture of textiles. Their sense of touch is very different. We are working with Italians on design production, and with a German construction company. Technical knowledge is not enough. I think that exploring existing cultures, cultures also of feeling, are certainly very efficient methods when seeking to create new and specific buildings and to increase our knowledge of this field. For me, Paco Rabanne has been a reference, as has Christian Lacroix's baroque feeling, John Galliano and Jean-Paul Gaultier.'

Perrault unfolds his image of the future city when he describes his view of what remains to be achieved in this way of designing and experiencing the space of such fabric–architectural concepts. His position also has a political dimension, for he aims for a more democratic, human and pleasurable type of space. His imagination seems simultaneously rational but playful, critical but practical and haunting when he speculates on the future:

'I want to create a new vision of architecture and the city. Finishing the Las Teresitas complex in Tenerife is the first step towards the creation of a geographical topography with meshes – it's a new vision of architecture. I would like to change the skyline of the city. In the history of architecture, the roof has always been significant. If you could change the idea of the roof and how it is used (one of the significant contributions of Modernism), to change the whole situation of the "roof" in the city, would be an important and strong new vision for the idea of the "skyline". Introducing a new relationship between the city, people and architecture,

Dominique Perrault, University of Seville Library and Research Centre, Seville, Spain, 2006
The shallow curving of the variably patterned panels for the exterior meshwork of this new research centre and library articulates the single, large, nave-like interior of the space with a shifting flux of shadows and mixing patterns.

Dominique Perrault, Innsbruck Town Hall, Austria, 2002
The play of light between the metallic fabrics and glass skin of the new town hall generates spectacular optical and moiré effects.

Dominique Perrault, Scottish Widows Tower, London, 2001
A wraparound net-curtain wall becomes a wrinkled dress for a tower. One of a series of conceptual computer-rendered sketches for the Scottish Widows headquarter's skyscraper in the City of London.

through textiles, would mean we could move and change the presence of architecture. This would transform the city with a more fashion-like feeling. To be able to buy a new exterior skin like we buy our clothes is an exciting dream. To be able to change the city, step by step through these kinds of changes in building envelopes would be interesting because it would accelerate architecture and its rate of change.

'But speed is not the only question or the unique problem. We should totally kill the idea that architecture is fixed, finished. Architecture can and should change, where it is needed. Architecture does not need to be closed, it can be in a continuous state of becoming. At present architecture and our relationship to it is very conservative and passive – it's not active. This is no longer enough. I can imagine buildings that change their garments to communicate their changing function or ownership, or other aspects of architecture, to make buildings fit more flexibly. My motive here, my life's work, is to make buildings you can touch and change fluidly. Architecture today is an authoritarian presence, but we could and should manipulate existing, past and future architecture.' Δ⊃

Notes
1. R Oldenburg, *The Great Good Place: Cafes, Coffee Shops, Bookstores, Bars, Hair Salons and the Other Hang-Outs at the Heart of a Community*, Marlowe & Company (New York), 1999.
2. Wolf D Prix, *Get Off of My Cloud*, Hatje Cantz (Germany), 2005.
3. A Betsky, 'From shaped space to the making of nothing: architecture and spatial planning in Late Capitalist Netherlands', in A Betsky and S Franke et al, *New Commitment in Architecture, Art and Design*, NAI (Rotterdam), 2003.
4. G DeBure, *Mesh*, W Editions (Paris), 2002.

Dominique Perrault, Las Teresitas, Tenerife, Spain, 2003
Computer rendering of the elevation of the complex. The entire mountain-like form of the hotel is swathed with a mesh that changes through the seasons as flowers and vegetation grow on its surface, connecting the building further into the geography of its site.

Blood Sense Tower, Deptford, London

Sally Quinn

Our increasingly elderly and ill population is finding healthy body products, such as blood, in shrinking supply because fewer people are in the age bracket within which they are able to donate. Already, blood is one of the most valuable commodities on earth, worth 1,675 times the value of refined petroleum. The proposal for the Blood Sense Tower, developed within the Masters of Architecture programme at the Royal College of Art, London, in 2003–04, is a monumental response to the increasing importance of accommodating London's future needs for a larger blood supply, and reflects the increasing economic, social and cultural importance of blood and organ donation.

Topped with a telecommunications needle, the 200-metre (656-foot) high tower facilitates and celebrates the market for harnessing, storing, servicing and distributing London's body products. It interweaves the activities of donors, laboratory staff and visitors with sterile mass-storage volumes preserving blood, sperm, ova and stem cells.

A corset exhibiting tubes of blood reappropriates the traditional tailoring technique of piping. This inversion translates into exposed seams within the building where the structure and occupation are made explicit. The relationship between the imposing structure and the delicate textures and forms of the corset are reflected in the techniques used to model, structure and construct the tower. Sac-like cryopreservation storage units are the dominant elements of the building and were modelled with knitted cotton stretched over a structural frame. Their fragile cellular texture is constructed largely with photovoltaic cladding panels connecting, through energy, the fabric of the building with the process of maintaining and preserving body products. Nesting into the pulsating storage volumes are public areas, visitor routes and donation spaces modelled with red raw silk. These potentially contaminated public spaces are detailed to be soft, sensual and intimate.

The Blood Sense Tower aims to inject into London a new social, medical and urban function. Its form and tectonics sew together surgical, textile and fashion aesthetics and techniques to give expression to a new architectural and urban typology. ∆

Sally Quinn

'Otherworldliness': The Pull of Black Velvet, Latex, Tights, Quilts, Tablecloths and Frocks

An Interview with Will Alsop

Will Alsop is most immediately identified with the expressive, colourful and painterly in architecture. His reputation as architecture's masterly Abstract Expressionist all too easily overshadows his engagement with more specific material and conceptual concerns. In conversation with Alsop at his Battersea studios, **Mark Garcia** discovered that a preoccupation with textiles has been latent in his work since his studies at the Architectural Association (AA) in the early 1970s. It is only, however, in a recent body of work that Alsop has started to innovatively bring it to the fore by translating the unexploited qualities of textiles into a plausible architecture.

As a first-year architecture student at the Architectural Association in London in the late 1960s, Will Alsop found a piece of black velvet and stuck it into his sketchbook. Intrigued by its sensuous and tactile qualities of light and texture the impression of these qualities have remained with him to this day, when he expresses concern over the lack of truly sensual and expressive urban design in the UK.

Alsop's generation of practical, spectacular and sculptural architecture has been linked to his fine-art-based research methods. His intimate, sensitive and tactile sketchbooks are just one component of a much broader range of methods he deploys in his search for new architectural ideas. The abstract, colourful, large-scale paintings, muscular, enigmatic and busy sketch models, organic and unpredictable presentation models and shocking plastic and maximalist computer images are just as important. When his working practices have been critically analysed, the focus has tended towards the obvious: tectonics, form, colour, texture and sensory effect. There have been few who have focused on the more specific material aspects of his design processes. In particular, his use of textiles has largely been ignored. Though multimedia and multidisciplinary in methodology, it is the textile aspects of Alsop's design processes that have recently matured and come to the fore in his recent work. His position in the meshwork between architecture and textiles is one of the more interesting due to the multidimensional, eclectic and lateral strategies he deploys.

Some of the origins of Alsop's interest in textiles lie in his education. As a first-year student at the AA he was taught structural systems by tutors like Keith Critchlow, Iain Pickering, Rob Underwood and Tony Dugdale. The three courses on offer at the time were tensegrity, pneumatics and tensile structures. Alsop became interested in all three and, he says, 'as a result I got interested in latex, but because it's unstable you can't use it for very much architecturally. I used it to make models because you could push it and pull it

Alsop Architects, West Queen West, Toronto, Canada, 2006
The facade of this residential tower was generated using a handcrafted textile and foam surface which was then digitised and applied, as a 3-D model, on to the striped volume of the building. Each housing unit is thereby detailed with its own nonrepeated pattern and unique visual identity.

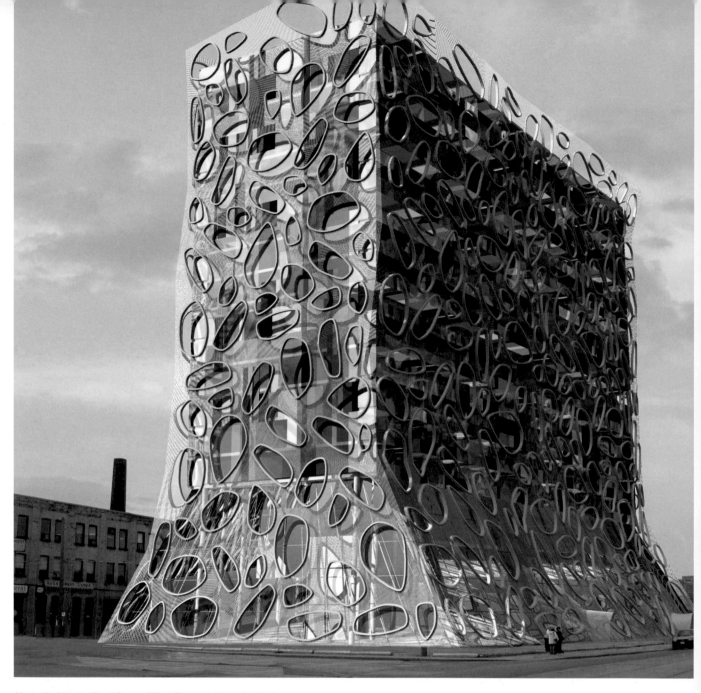

Alsop Architects, West Queen West, Toronto, Canada, 2006
A double layering of stripes on the internal skin plays against the variable holes in the external mesh of the outer surface of the building.

in interesting ways. But now you can use new materials to build those types of models.'

Alsop demonstrates a curious ability in being able to identify a considerable quantity of these architecturally unexploited textile properties and in translating them effectively and innovatively into a plausible architecture. Textiles enable him to use and explore the spatial meaning of words and qualities like 'ruche', 'cosy' and 'tablecloth', terms absent from most architectural discourse or practice. He uses the emotions of comfort and cosiness when referring to the importance of creating a 'nest-like barrier between your environment and the outside world'. Projects like the recent Fawood School, the Spiky Pod (inside the Queen Mary Westfield biomedical research laboratories), Commonwealth

Institute and the Stonebridge Hat (all in London), and the new residential high-rises in Bangkok (Bangkok Balcony Bash) and Toronto (West Queen West), all treat architectural space with such ideas in mind.

New developments in textile materials technologies, CAD and CAM processes and engineering are now allowing Alsop to build his quixotic forms, such as the Spiky Pod. As he notes, 'now that we have better-elasticated fabrics we can build the models. The particular fabric we used for Spiky allows you to make these extreme points. What I was looking for there was to create these very peculiar objects floating above what can be a fairly prosaic, but often important, activity – working in a laboratory. The effect is that while working on what might be the resolution of something like cancer, another world hovers above you. The two things are related. Inside the pods are seminar rooms, unusually wrapped up because I think seminar rooms should be quite interesting places. The centre of the cell is based on the form of a cancerous cell, but Spiky is not accurately based on anything from biology, though it does have that sort of germ-like quality. It looks threatening, like many of the things the medical researchers in the building deal with.

'Much of my work has been involved with the use of external skins over unusual things inside. To make Spiky in any other way outdoors would be extremely expensive, but to make it in a tailor-made elastic fabric is relatively simple. So you can imagine its origins as being a sphere from which you just pull pieces out, and that is what you end up with. When you sit inside, it means that the totality of the external skin goes all the way around you and creates another world. The relative hardness of the platform gives another sense of enclosure within this slightly threatening external skin.'

An interesting fact about Spiky is that the sketch model was made from a humble foam ball, some pencils and a pair of tights. Many architects believe the computer is the only way to create innovative, complex and advanced forms, but Alsop believes that 'the idea of playing around with bits of fabric and a model is still very productive. It is nonsense that if you are not adept at the computer you can't produce innovative forms or architecture. When my students at the University of Vienna produce tensile structures they get excited about Frei Otto. This is a sign that these types of structures and ways of working are exciting, but tend to be characterised as "one of those". They are usually rather banal and look forlorn, but they don't have to be. It's just that no one has really taken them very far. It would be great to do Spiky on a large scale as an external skin.'

Spiky has been referred to in the media as the world's most complex tensile structure. The seamless way in which its 360-degree form integrates the complex double structural system (both compression and tensile) is significant and original. The project has opened up further possibilities for Alsop, who intends to take the principles demonstrated in Spiky further. The completely 3-D wraparound skin of an early version of his C-Plex (now the Public) in West Bromwich, Birmingham, is an indicator of how this might be realised.

Alsop Architects, Bangkok Tower, Bangkok, 2004
Top: The physical sketch model of the skin for the tower was made by using wire shaped into rounded frames around which a translucent textile was ruched. Bottom: This second stage in the skin development process translated the ruched textile model into a digital 3-D surface model. A number of contrasting patterns were then rendered on to more complex deformations of the facade's topography.

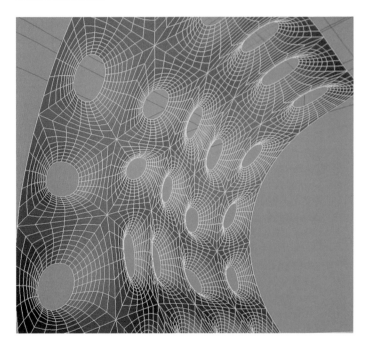

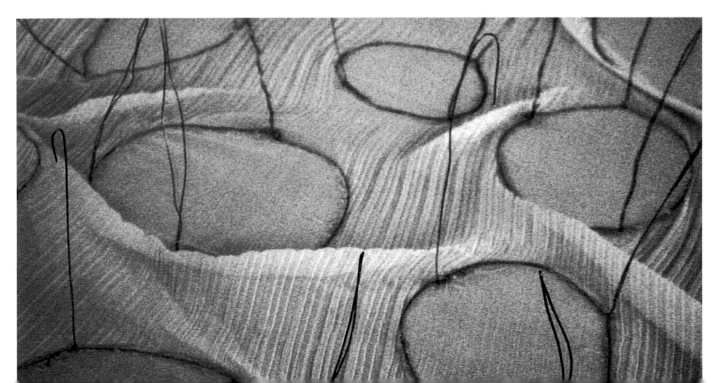

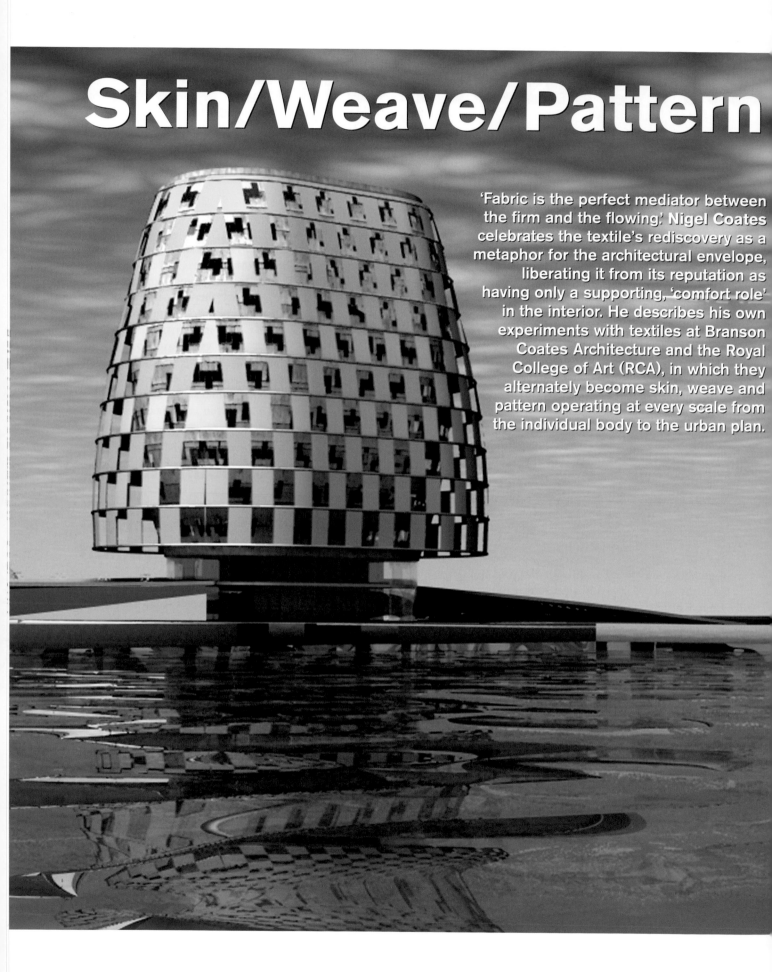

Skin/Weave/Pattern

'Fabric is the perfect mediator between the firm and the flowing.' **Nigel Coates** celebrates the textile's rediscovery as a metaphor for the architectural envelope, liberating it from its reputation as having only a supporting, 'comfort role' in the interior. He describes his own experiments with textiles at Branson Coates Architecture and the Royal College of Art (RCA), in which they alternately become skin, weave and pattern operating at every scale from the individual body to the urban plan.

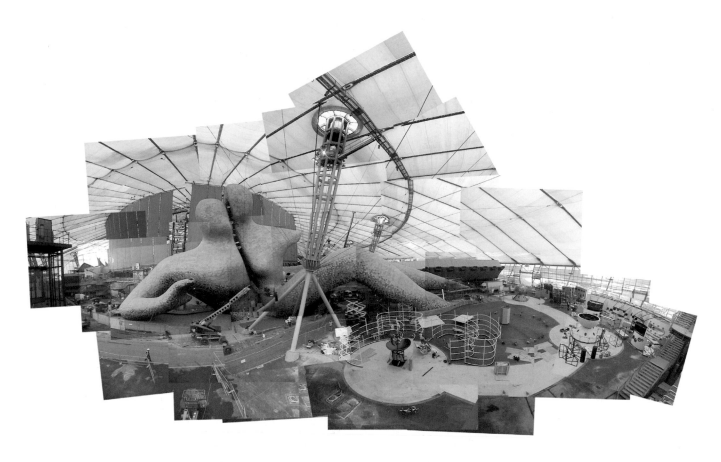

Branson Coates Architecture, Body Zone, Millennium Dome, London, 1999
Though a hybrid of male and female, the Body Zone was first and foremost a building with a continuous tiled surface.

Whether relentless blocks or cosy cottages, most forms of domestic architecture need a little humanising, and it is here that fabric can sometimes provide the answer. Apart from the upholstered cover on the chair or the linen on the bed, curtains and blinds blur the harshness of window openings, and carpets soften floors. In their many woven forms, textiles play their part in shaping architecture from both practical and cultural points of view. But, instead of hiding indoors as textiles have traditionally done, and fulfilling the comfort role, they are now often seen as a conceptual tool for a dynamic new kind of building.

Apart from in the case of tents and tensiles, which have a perfectly reasonable architectural history of their own, using the textile as a metaphor for the architectural envelope is relatively recent. We are now considering textiles exactly because they bend and curve, and can mould themselves to form as the skin does to the body. The seamed and tailored textile surface can continue uninterrupted, and link the inside with the outside.

Since architects discovered the *The Fold*,[1] Deleuze's avariciously consumed study of pliant surface, they have used the textile as a conceptual tool for liberating form from the usual constraints. The conceptual framework of the fold emphasises the voluptuous surface as opposed to the pure and (inherently) rational structure, and the textile is its most direct material. The textile can defy gravity, and appear to float. It moves with air, and is the antithesis of architectural support. For instance, the magic carpet supports the rider, but is itself not supported by any visible means, whereas loose fabric folds that wrap the female body respond to her dance and a gentle breeze.

It is ironic, then, that fabric has always been represented in sculpted stone, and been a favourite rhetorical exaggeration of a continuous masonry surface. You can carve stone into anything – plants, animals or swathes of brocade. The draped tunics of the Elgin marbles help their figural composition within the tympanum, and the architecture adopts a dynamic interface with the body. Fabric, it seems, is the perfect mediator

Branson Coates Architecture, Minnie-Crinnie, Middlehaven, Middlesbrough, Teesside, 2005
Alsop's master plan called for a response to his Prada skirt idea, and the result was an office building with a crinoline that acts as a brise-soleil.

Gianlorenzo Bernini, *Estasi di Santa Teresa*, Capella Cornaro, Santa Maria della Vittoria, Rome, 1647–52
Looking into the folds in Teresa's skirts reveals the clue to baroque architecture.

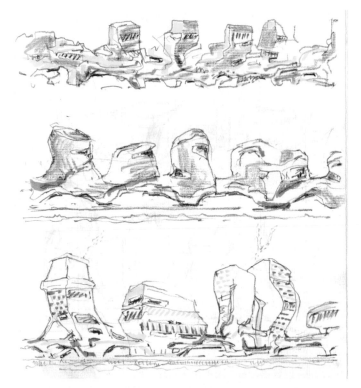

Branson Coates Architecture, New Wapping, Silvertown, east London, 2006
Digital techniques have enabled stretching and separating to be applied directly to planning large areas of the city, like this one at the mouth of the River Lee.

between the firm and the flowing, between the fixed rational world of masonry and the ephemeral life it must support.

As though the statue was itself an architectural manifesto, the voluptuous folds in Bernini's Santa Teresa's habit reinforce the dynamics of the chapel (Capella Cornaro) within which it is the focus, and are the key to baroque architecture. One might think of the church, Santa Maria della Vittoria, and everything in it, as one continuous textile with neither seams nor tears. We are inside the stomach of a giant's body, where an organic lining unites the disparate parts, of walls, floors and ceilings, cherubs and crosses and bursts of light, and only gradually transforms as it passes over these. In a loaded environment like this, the textile idea helps lift its narrative into an abstract, ethereal and united state.

Architects (myself included) have understandably been eager to apply digital working methods to rework baroque ideas of experiential flow, unity between opposites, connection, movement and antigravity. We've found that virtual meshes can be stretched and distorted into irregular or organic forms. The downside of the digital model is that it reduces folded forms to surfaces. But when you consider surface as a textile, it regains a conceptual depth, and upgrades to a genuine architectural condition. With the textile manifold, Baroque has been revived in a freer form, beyond the limitations of masonry.

Textile As Skin
Some years ago, when John Galliano still showed in London and was experimenting with deconstruction and bias cutting, he asked me for some architectural plans to turn into a dress. I'd just finished our first building in Japan – the Ark in Sapporo. He took the plans and deliberately ignored their architectural content. Printed on a fine felt-like fabric with no stretch, he cut pieces like paper and laid them on top of one another to make the shape. It aroused my interest in the connection between paper and the way a dress is cut; paper is the beginning of just about any garment pattern. The paper pattern has an architectural quality in that it uses a nonstretch flexible surface to make completely 3-D forms as a result of the way flat components are seamed together. He made me realise that architecture could learn more from clothing.

At Branson Coates Architecture (BCA), the firm's competition design for a new wing at the Royal College of Art in London proved an ideal project to invert Galliano's idea and apply the language of clothing to a building. We began by taking a conventional jacket pattern and, at model scale, made a set of tiny maquettes in calico. Each one was then stiffened, and by laying them on their sides they were used to make an architectural model. The jacket of each floor was rotated in relation to the next, and various details in them given architectural roles. The sleeve on one of the jackets became a stair, and a smaller jacket standing vertically at the corner of the building became the entrance.

Although the design process had started by using actual fabric, the project had certain contradictions. The clothing pattern had helped define the form of the building, but it emerged as a rigid, nondirectional surface that had lost the seamed panels amid a sea of tiles. More had to be learnt about how to make a body-like space, and to experiment with skin and textile becoming one condition.

When designing the Body Zone in the Millennium Dome, BCA's aim was to make a statement that was simultaneously spectacular and as unassuming as hopefully we are about our own bodies. As the design developed in a to-and-fro process of physical modelling, computer scanning, functional scaling and rapid prototyping, it became evident that the skin defined the relationship between the appearance of the object and the experience of being inside it. Besides the bifurcated twins of the male and female that made up the single figure, the skin would be next in its hierarchy of signifiers.

Clearly the Body Zone was dealing with repetition, pattern and decorative surface, but it was also textile-like because of its incremental structure and the adaptation of the square component of the lenticular plastic tile to a complex curving surface. It shares this elemental textile principle with Future Systems' Selfridges in Birmingham. Its standardised dots adapt their linkages to both give a textile-like continuity and model the surface to wrap the building's curves in such a way as to read as a skin. Both Selfridges and the Body Zone use primary surfaces to mask the complexities of what lies behind them.

Skin has the quality of adapting and stretching, but ultimately it needs flesh and bone to support it. It is true that some textiles are so close to the body that they become a second skin, and on other occasions it is the distance between body and textile surface that makes them wearable. Some work best because of their fine weave, and others on their looseness and ability to breathe.

The definition of a textile might be a woven combination of threads that pass one above the other. A textile can never be totally two-dimensional. Unlike a digitally generated surface, and more like a textile, together the threads bond into a continuous condition with substance and, therefore, thickness. This thickness may be analogous to the skin on our bodies, but it is also comparable to the substance of the city, of the depth of construction occupied by buildings, sewers and roads.

Textile As Weave

When a fabric is stretched across the bias, the relationship between the warp and the weft shifts to the diagonal. This technique can be applied to an architectural plan, and pulled towards an elongated form. Zaha Hadid does this compulsively, as though the bias technique were the driver in her work. The pulling and distorting occurs not so much in the buildings as they are realised, but in the process through which they are designed. Even in the predigital phases of her work, with projects like the Hong Kong Peak, she used a continuous textile condition to subject the entire urban landscape to the eye of the beholder.

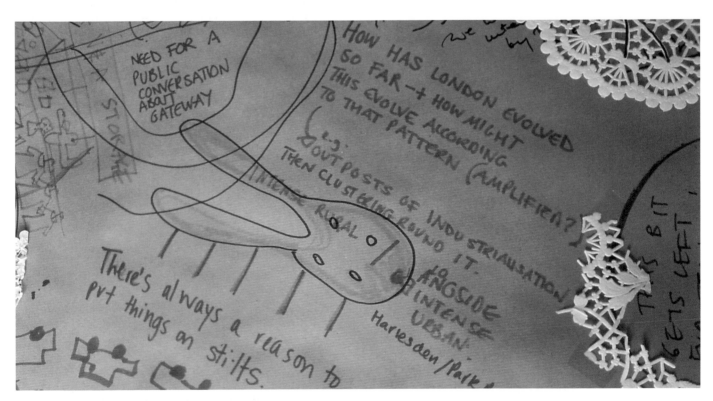

G4 (Will Alsop, Sam Jacob, Tom Coward, Nigel Coates), First Thames Gateway Workshop, Royal College of Art, London, 2006
As part of a series of G4 collaborative design workshops held around London, the Thames Gateway master-planning workshop resulted in the making of this visualisation of the ongoing conversation where each participant responded to the moves of the others.

Nigel Coates, E-voluton, Rainham Marsh, Essex, 2005
Including Nest and Raspberry Park: identity needs to be built into the local DNA, and what better way to see the evidence than from the air.

Just about any aerial photo of London reveals a matrix of roads, railways and walkways threaded above and below one another. The city is so layered and woven that some designer might have had a hand in planning it. However, for the most part there was no such overview. This textural interpretation, quite literally urban fabric, was the starting point for a recent BCA project called New Wapping, near Silvertown in east London, at the mouth of the River Lee. Around the area,

motorways and railways duck and dive like warp and weft. Within the site, however, the key was to potato-print urban fabric taken from two other parts of London. Shoreditch and Wapping were chosen as examples of urban regeneration based on the reuse of the warehouse building. These were stretched and bias-cut to fit the model areas in such a way that they retained some of their original character, while drawing in the features of the surrounding areas. On the periphery of the project, a second level of paths and connections snakes between the buildings. These two levels define interconnected territories between which paths and stairs make linkages analogous to weave. Occasionally a single thread gets pulled upwards into a surface knot that stands out as a building.

Any urban plan carries the risk of curtailing three-dimensional thinking. But if the buildings have an inherent relationship with the 'thickness' of the plan, then plan, section and elevation might merge into a single three-dimensional condition. Instead of buildings being component parts of the urban fabric, they can be seen as agglomerations of threads that coincide to make inhabitable spaces. Any one surface of a building can extend outwards to the public realm or slide upwards on to the surface of another structure. Similarly, the interweaving breaks down in scale. Each thread consists of a number of yarns, whether tightly or loosely twisted. If you took the microscope to these, you would find doors and windows, beams and columns.

While New Wapping is still relatively open-ended, and its threads as multivarious as the city itself, BCA's Mini-Crinnie building in the Middlehaven area of Middlesbrough in Teesside bears closer inspection in terms of depth and weave. The idea here was to develop a deep woven surface that resembles tweed. The combination of colours, materials and weave give the impression of a knotty three-dimensional surface. Its inner skin, and the one that defines the environmental barrier between inside and outside, is a torso-like form with a dogtooth fenestration pattern. With only 30 per cent of the surface being glazed, environmentalists will spot Part-L (energy-saving building regulations) compliance. Together with the wooden shingles that complete it, the window pattern establishes a woven character. But the view of the inner surface will always be oblique because it is masked (or added to) by a structure that hangs from the upper edge, or waist, of the building.

With intermediary pink and orange fabric strips, a giant crinoline obscures the inner surface both visually and from the sun. From inside the building the outward view will be modulated though not obscured; the shading fabric has a coarse enough weave to allow views through it. The combination of inner and outer surfaces, of shingle skin and fabric crinnie, unites two essentially separate rhythms into a deep 'tweedy' surface. And like so many woven patterns in nature, the one on the Minnie-Crinnie adapts incrementally (or algorithmically) to the curved form it covers.

Textile As Pattern

At an early G4 workshop,[2] four of the group's members crowded around a table covered in brown paper. To define the subject of the exercise as the Thames Gateway, one of us drew in the rope-like signature of the River Thames. As our ideas gathered pace, writing spewed on to the canvas from all sides. Interestingly, in the absence of the usual pattern provided by maps or architectural drawing, the humble paper doily found its way on to the board and got used as an abstract sign for metropolitan intensity.

These qualities have everything and nothing to do with the future town, and this is why they are useful. It is as though tenets on decoration have reversed. Rather than being integrated, the pattern has outgrown its constraints of scale, and can now exploit a separation from its context. As it becomes easier to print digitally at any size, and on just about any surface, the disjunction between material and pattern means that pattern itself can be an active element of architectural composition.

E-volve, a 2005 research project for the Thames Gateway,[3] made strategic use of pattern from the start. It included patterns representing distinct cultures, at a variety of scales, and others collaged or patchworked on to the landscape like the planned fragments that make up the suburbia surrounding British cities. This project was aiming for contrast as well as continuity.

The notion of the evolving city needs structures that maintain a sense of flux, so the intention in E-volve, or E-voluton as it came to be known, was to contrast the intensely urban areas located on top of hills with the fields and marsh around them. Land and building alike play their part in defining the architecture, as does the Italian hill town in relation to the land around it. Two of E-voluton's autonomous neighbourhoods, Nest and Paisley, capture the psycho-geographic identity of these places with their concentric, decorative plans. The surrounding land carries a panoply of other patterns, each bearing a particular cultural mark; tartan coexists with paisley and a digital mesh.

This massive remnant quilt corresponds to the treatment of floors inside the apartment blocks in the area. Instead of one floor pattern being chosen for each interior, E-voluton residents mix the tile patterns as though they have bought end-of-line bargains in B&Q. As well as defining boundaries they blur them, and help define a narrative lexicon. The balcony tiles are based on the plan of my imaginary city, Ecstacity – they put the entire city underfoot. In the film version of the project,[4] the featured living interior changes as new occupants arrive. New patterns help define the territorial conditions and minimise the need for walls.

With digital technologies we have the means to build, print or cut at any scale, from the town as a whole, to walls that divide and enclose, to the things people use in their living spaces. The Fiorella lamp I designed recently turned out to have an ideal outline for a green space. The data used to laser-cut its original prototype was easy to transfer to the plan of Raspberry Park on E-voluton's riverside. Each of its giant flowers would translate into a clump of trees. From the ground the park would have the mysterious qualities of a naturally seeded wood, but if coming in to land at London City Airport, one would read its pattern as a giant urban hieroglyph.

Narrative can be injected into a project through the medium of the programme, but it can also contradict it and be a collection of referential fragments that hover between form and meaning. You can collage narrative, or build into a patchwork paradigm of the functional. In the context of the textile manifold, the phenomenon of pattern is well placed to supply the cultural depth the Thames Gateway might need. The textile phenomenon in architecture gives us the means to orchestrate narrative form and function in new ways that combine abstraction and mood rather than specific reference or prescribed experience. ⌂

Notes
1. Gilles Deleuze, *The Fold: Leibniz and the Baroque*, University of Minnesota Press, 1992.
2. G4 is the affiliated group of architectural practices SMC Alsop, Branson Coates Architecture, FAT and Agents of Change.
3. The project is the result of a collaboration between the Royal College of Art and Branson Coates Architecture, led/designed by Nigel Coates.
4. A film of the E-voluton project was exhibited at the Avenirs de Ville exhibition in Nancy in 2005.

Holon Design Museum, Israel

Ron Arad Associates

In 2003, Ron Arad Associates was invited by the Municipality of Holon, Israel, to design and develop a new Design Museum for the city. The designated site for the £6 million museum (due to open late 2007) occupies a 3,200-square-metre (34,445-square-foot) (net area) plot, and its gentle, plateau-like topography was to be articulated by the arrangement of the museum facilities over two staggered levels.

The greater part of the museum's external appearance is shrouded by five dominant ribbons of Corten steel that undulate and meander their way in, out and around the building's internal volumes, at times in unison, at others apart; at times enclosing space, and at times notionally defining it. The ribbons act as a spine for the building, both supporting it structurally and dictating its posture in relation to its surroundings. The horizontality of their layout is further accentuated by a gentle and natural patination of the steel over the lifetime of the building, both of which echo the topographic notion of the open Israeli terrain in the urban context.

As the structural ribbons encircle the museum's west wing and reach the inner courtyard, they begin to splay apart and project vertically beyond the upper edge of the main gallery on the first floor, spanning the entire plaza in midair, only to reunite over the circulation ramp and proceed to frame the gallery and support it at a 7-metre (23-foot) height over the ground below.

The 480-square-metre (5,167-square-foot) gallery will harness Israel's consistent natural lighting potential and be lit via a 'corduroy' of light reflectors in the ceiling. The ribbons' apparent acrobatics also act as a visual key to a visitor's position within the museum and provide partial shading during the hottest hours of the day. *D*

Ron Arad

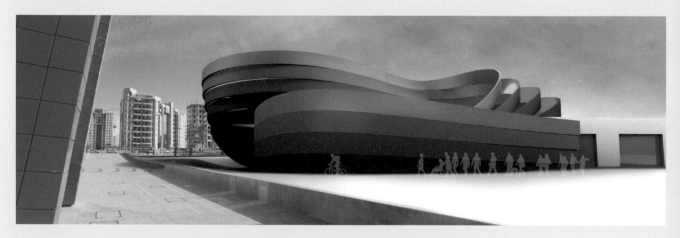

Lister Mills, Bradford

David Morley Architects

The penthouses have a plaited form similar to woven yarn.

Velvet Mill is one of two imposing 19th-century Grade II* listed structures at the Lister Mills complex in Manningham, Bradford, built by Samuel Cunliffe Lister between 1870 and 1873. The textile mill thrived until its 1970s decline and, finally, closure in 1990, lying vacant and vandalised until 1999 when Urban Splash, in partnership with Bradford City Council, Yorkshire Forward and English Heritage, rescued the site.

The roof offers huge potential to express the building's new residential use and regenerate Manningham and Bradford. The mill is a robust stone building complemented by the lightness and delicacy of the proposed penthouses, which will have a matt-silver metal roof, clear glazing and glass doors to timber-decked balconies. Up close, the roof will recede, but from further away its plait-like appearance will be more legible, resembling woven yarn. The two modular wings are symmetrical about the existing central stair tower, which will continue to dominate the skyline of the mill.

The penthouses evoke a curvilinear metal fabric wrapped into a plait. At the fold lines the double-curved modules are separated by glazed slots over the staircases. This rigorous geometry enables diagonal views towards the city and the hills. The two storeys can be configured as scissor duplexes with the bedrooms on the east-facing side and living rooms on the west, or vertical stacked duplexes or single-level apartments with dual-aspect upper floors. The living areas on the upper levels are characterised by the curved soffit that describes the form of the modules.

The form of the roof has been modelled using cutting-edge parametric 3-D computer software, so is a truly contemporary design, bringing new life to a handsome old structure. Each part has its own integrity and Lister, a consummate innovator, would no doubt have supported the planning approval for the project, received in July this year. △

David Morley and Danielle Tinero

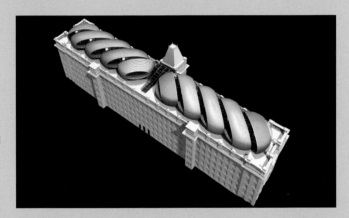

Aerial view of Velvet Mill showing the proposed penthouses. The modules have a double-curved form clad in a ribbed or standing-seam metal sheet material that further evokes the texture of woven yarn. The geometry was developed with engineer Tim Lucas of Price & Myers 3d Engineering.

Courtyard view. The robustness and solidity of the stone-mill building is complemented by the lightness and delicacy of the glass and metal penthouses. From ground level, the penthouses appear to float as they recede from view and reflect the colour of the sky.

Textile Tectonics
An Interview with Lars Spuybroek

'Architectural design is not about having ideas, but about having techniques, techniques that operate on a material level. It's about making matter think and live by itself.' Here Lars Spuybroek of NOX talks to **Maria Ludovica Tramontin** about his engagement with the work of Gottfried Semper and Frei Otto and how it has led him to his own brand of textile tectonics or 'soft constructivism', in which textiles are transformed into the tectonic through conventional textile techniques – weaving, bundling, interlacing, braiding, knitting or knotting – effectively building structure through softness and flexibility.

NOX's interest in textiles conjugates the in-depth exploration of both Frei Otto and Gottfried Semper, one introducing textile into architecture through the physical realm of engineering, the other through the symbolic realm of style. In this sense we should understand NOX's operations between computed curves as research into systems able to integrate the surface suppleness with structural toughness, to use Semper's terms.[1] NOX has received international recognition for its research on the relationship between architecture and computing. Working with computed curves – splines – has always been a mixture of analogue and digital. One is always pervading the other: textile techniques become computing techniques, surface becomes structure, and structure becomes geometry. It goes beyond a pure transmutation of textile techniques into design techniques; it is, as Lars Spuybroek would say, a completely 'textile way of thinking' in architecture. In NOX's projects textile intervenes at different levels, either at the purely aesthetic level of undulating surfaces, or at the structural level of weaving and braiding of steel members, or at the methodological level of using techniques 'instead of ideas' to generate architectural form.

In the Maison Folies cultural complex in Lille (2001–04), the spectacular glimmering facade is a eulogy to Semper's *Bekleidungsprinzip*, a supple ornate surface draped over a tectonic volume. In addition, the designs for the European Central Bank in Frankfurt (2003) and the Seoul Opera House (2005) are not just aesthetic surfaces, they are also structured as heavy nets, and are closer to the notions of Frei Otto. Then, deploying Otto's techniques of analogue computing, NOX used actual woollen threads to generate the complex interlacing of towers for the design of the new World Trade Center in New York, or the utopian Situationist urbanism of ParisBRAIN, or the structural weaving of paper strips in the public artwork of Son-O-House. Finally, using digital techniques for the later projects like the Jalisco Library or the Jeongok Prehistory Museum, we find a fully Semperian notion of textile becoming architectural style.

Semper and Textile Tectonics
Spuybroek's reference to Semperian 'textile tectonics' appears in his book *NOX: Machining Architecture* and in his essay in Bernard Tschumi's *Architecture at the Beginning of the 21st Century*. For Spuybroek, the term has a number of distinct meanings:

'Above all, "textile tectonics" refers to Semper's adoration of textile and his four elements of architecture, being earth for foundation, wood for construction, textile for enclosure and fire for climate. It's such a beautiful way of ordering, from heavy to light, not being a pure materialism of built forms, but more like the Greek earth, water, air and fire, the

constituent elements that make up all the other materials and life forms. Semper's concept of textile drives everything, it's the main productive element, the main agent of architectural form. Not at all in the sense of masking, but in the sense of the woven wall being the *Urtechnik*, the original technique of making architecture. Architectural design is not about having ideas, but about having techniques, techniques that operate on a material level. It's about making matter think and live by itself. A concept that Semper is famous for is the *Stoffwechselthese*, the transformation of materials, which means buildings aren't made of textile any more, but that textile has been transmaterialised into stone and steel and other constituent parts. So, it's not so much ideas that inhabit matter, but other materials. Textile inhabiting stone. Materials in materials, I find that astonishing. It's an abstract materialism, saving us from idealism and realism at the same time. He was very conscious of that, he wanted to steer in between "speculative aesthetics" and "mere engineering". But it is a very active, evolutionary materialism, a vitalism almost, especially when you remember *Stoffwechsel* is German for metabolism. Literally it means "change of substance" and even more literally, "change of fabric"!'

The Semperian Reversal
Spuybroek's critical notion of the 'Semperian reversal' has been central to his research focus into 'textile tectonics' and his work radically updates and goes beyond Semper. For Spuybroek, the significance of this reversal lies in its interest in 'a pure *Bekleidungsprinzip*, to see if the principle of incrustation can be fully merged with the one of dressing. I'd like the hardening to run parallel with adornment, as with the double meaning of the English word "make-up". It's not always so clear with Semper whether he is making a consistent distinction between structure and ornament; between the wooden scaffolding and the woven wall. But since these are categories, not real materials, stone enacts the role of both. Semper is very articulate on the tradition of incrustation as not simply decorative and he says that "art form and decoration are so intimately related that it is impossible to consider them in separated views". To make it overly clear, I call it a reversal, but that is a reversal of the *order* of the four elements, where the tectonic precedes the textile, I want the *textile to become tectonic itself*. In that case the soft elements become rigid through collaboration, by teaming up, by weaving, bundling, interlacing, braiding, knitting or knotting and through that convolution the whole becomes strong and rigid. That's also why I call it a soft constructivism, which has nothing to do with hard materials mimicking softness or liquidity, but with softness and flexibility building structure.'

NOX, Son-O-House, Son en Breugel, the Netherlands, 2000–04
The final structure of this public artwork commissioned by Industrieschap Ekkersrijt was developed and built in collaboration with the Engineers Bollinger + Grohmann (Germany) and SFL (Austria).

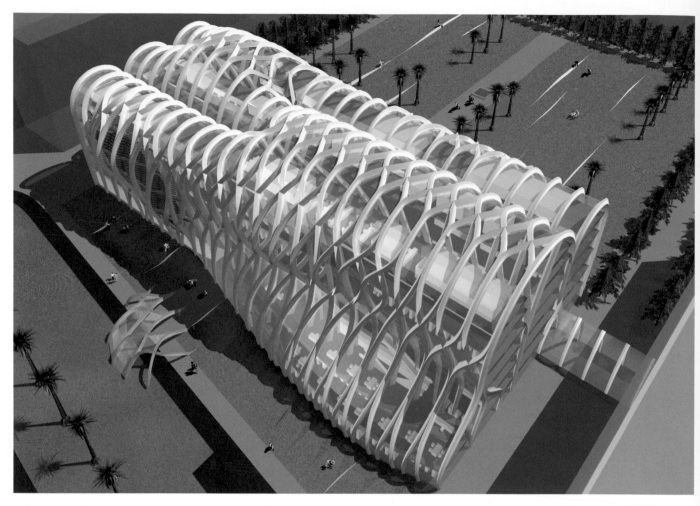

NOX, Jalisco Library, Guadalajara, Mexico, competition entry 2005
The practice's textile operations on structural members have brought the architects very close to a new understanding of Gothic configurations. Spuybroek is especially interested in Gothics as 'an architecture of continuity' following the ideas of Wilhelm Worringer who described Gothics as 'vitalised geometry'.

Softness and Hardness

Omnipresent in the criticism of Spuybroek's designs is the observation that his architecture only looks soft but is in fact hard. For Spuybroek:

'There is no weak form, there is only soft architecture of hard form. What is architecture? Organisation. I always criticised going from the hard to the hard, like with grids or typology, where an archive of forms directly provides you with the necessary building. There is no morphogenesis, there is just replication. Morphogenesis and Constructivism all run simultaneously and together. The true reverse is a bottom-up process, and a bottom-up process inherently means Constructivism. Constructivism is something other than Constructionism or High Tech; it involves a final product as the result of a process, and since that is a material process it is constructed while it is formed, not afterwards by Arup. My buildings don't look like they are sagging or melting; it's actually the reverse. They are rising up, coming out of a process where flexible, textile elements have just hardened

into a form. It's hard, just not crystallised. It's difficult to see this distinction between sagging and rising up and we aren't helped by all the other topological architecture either, most of which is just rounded-off Modernism or rounded-off Deconstructivism.'

The Scalarity and Modelling of Textile Tectonics

Spuybroek's morphogenetic processes involve a complex set of scalar manoeuvres which translate forms using textile techniques across digital and physical means. These unique processes and the resulting materialities and geometries are crucial to an understanding of his research. When asked about how he generates interlacing across scales, from the surface to the structure and to massing, he explains that:

'We need to consider whether the microtectonics of the textile surface can become the macrotectonics of the edifice. Obviously, this is a reference to Frei Otto's analogue computing techniques where soft, movable, flexible elements, not just soap film or paper or sand, but even literally wool

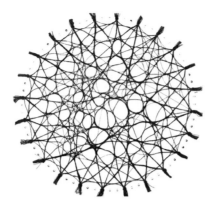

Frei Otto's analogue computing model of an optimised path system based on the slack of wool threads. The wool threads self-organise into a complex network after being dipped in water.

Gottfried Semper's illustration of knotted fabric.

threads, find each other and then collectively rigidify, find form. We should remember that analogue computing is exactly this materials-inhabiting-other-materials, a soap film on one scale can become a steel roof on the other scale. In my book *NOX: Machining Architecture* (2004) there are two iconographic images on the contents page: the wool-thread model by Frei Otto and next to that Semper's piece of knotted cloth. Frei Otto taught me that movement is not enough to generate complexity in architectural structures, even if our interest lies mainly with dynamic systems. First one needs a framework in which the movement takes place, a framework of flexibility, of variation, which is however typologically constrained. Second, next to movement being processed by that system, we need consolidation – you cannot just "freeze frame" movement; that is fake complexity, but not structure. In Frei Otto's machines, his analogue computers, a system *self-stops* through transformation. It transforms from soft to hard, but at the same moment from simple to complex. All these machines operate on physical slack and curvability becoming structural redundancy, movement becoming structure. I worked for a long time with these techniques but found that the variations were too diverse, the ranges of curvature too large. Textile techniques like the ones I described above – crochet, macramé, braiding, knitting, weaving – do something similar to morphogenesis, but in a more controlled manner. They produce similar structural nets but the interrelating of the flexible elements is much more controlled, top-down and bottom-up alternate in a much more frequent manner and produce a very aesthetic result. The types of curvature – what we call "figures" – are less divergent and simply more stylistic. In short, I would say that textile techniques are closer to what makes an architectural result.'

In Spuybroek's work we can see interlacing return on many different scales, from the surface to the structure, even to massing. He is clear on the ways in which this concept operates in his design process and explains that:

'In design, lines can exist on so many levels. Lines can be dashed or dotted centre lines that organise a whole band-like row of rooms or floors, they can be the continuous line that indicates much smaller elements like walls, beams or columns, or delineating the contours of elements like panels. The lines resulting from a textile design technique don't necessarily have to end up fully materialised in the final architectural object, they can flicker between organisational and structural. In 3-D modelling the relationship between line, surface and volume is completely different from that in drawing or sketching. In sketching you are always depicting, tracing. With a computer you are building the model. There are two types of lines, lines that are profiles, and lines that are rails. You can have a line that is extruded into a tube or an H-beam; you can have a line that can be lofted with another line to form a surface. As well as the generative textile techniques, we have the technology of the software which, taken together, make it a design technique.

'There is this constant vibration of real and abstract, a real textile technology can become a technique within another, digital technology, which then inhabits a building technology of steel and concrete and other materials. When Semper spoke of his *Stoffwechselthese* the textile weavings and bundles were carved from the stone, so there is a shift from one technique or style to another technique. But that is not a linear progressive relationship; both techniques inform the style, which becomes an abstract zone between two real, material states. For Semper a textile technique like weaving only made sense because there was a stone technique like carving. Nowadays we have to create our own transitions. For instance, steel can be bent or torqued, but not bent *and* torqued, meaning a three-dimensional spline can become a round tube, or a composite truss of two or three round tubes, but never an H-beam. A three-dimensional spline has to be subdivided into smoothly connected circle segments, second-degree curves. But keep in mind that each circle segment is flat. Therefore, to make the curve three-dimensional, the next circle segment should be rotated orthogonal to the shared tangent. This can only be done with a tube, not with an H-beam. It's just a single example and there are many like it.

NOX, Pompidou II, competition entry, Metz, France, 2003
Strapped balloon models were deployed for the structure and form generation of NOX's Pompidou II. The black bands indicate the position of structural elements.

There is a lot of information preserved in the material states of products. Never forget we design with products, and that information should be interfaced through geometry and technology. We now have the option to move towards half-products, to make the process more nonstandard, but this is limited for now to cutting, milling and moulding techniques. I find it striking that Semper's shift from weaving to stereotomy can now be one from weaving to milling foam for moulds. What is different here is that in his time stereotomy could take care of a whole monolithic section of the wall. We will always need to consider a *composite* assemblage, where panellisation immediately affects substructure and structure. Techniques, technology and geometry should always be

considered as having effects on each other and not as disparate. What I find problematic is that digital design in most schools considers that abstract zone as a playground only but not as an interface between two material states.'

Figure-Configuration Techniques
The textile techniques Spuybroek operates with are a subset of what he refers to as figure-configuration techniques:

'These configurations are often already close to a typology. A flat carpet for one-storey buildings, a strand for larger blocks or a vertical strand for towers. Figures are figures of movement, configurations are patterns of structure. The configurations always start out quite homogeneous, almost like a curved version of Dutch Structuralism, which is not what we want. If you consider a continuum of solid form on one side of the spectrum and liquid rhythms on the other, configuration is right next to form. I would like to have it closer to liquid, more like blocks of rhythms, resonating patterns.

'We allow for the homogeneous versions only as "tight", to start the design procedures with, then we always develop them towards a looser set-up, or towards combinations of loose and tight. If you just take the figures as immaterial lines, they behave like any other modular system or grid. Bringing in looseness helps to bring the materiality of the line back, and adds sliding-along to locking-in by increasing the variability of the curve. Since all these systems are parametric they are based on variability, and variability is based on interlaced curvature. What the design of textile techniques gives us is a precision that goes far beyond metaphor. Some architects nowadays refer to their spaces as "woven", which

The Metz project, seen from the large square, shows all double-curved shell areas in white translucent epoxy and single-curved portal areas in stainless steel.

NOX, Jeongok Prehistory Museum, competition entry (honourable mention), Jeongok Gyeonggi-do, South Korea, 2005
NOX's museum seen from the front reveals how the Semperian concept of textile drives the variation of volume, of structure and fenestration.

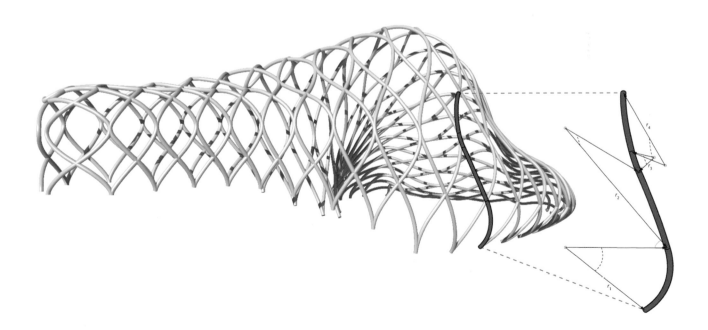

The structure for the museum is based on rolled steel tubes. All 3-D curves consist of flat circle segments.

they simply are not. These textile techniques allow you to regulate the amount of realisation, to be precise with the weaving itself but to be more vague with the actual component or element that is woven (eg floor, structure, panels or combinations of these). It doesn't necessarily mean that all the steel needs to be woven, or all the circulation. I prefer any technique to start with nesting itself between everything, and allowing it potentially to affect everything. But we should be careful to not make it *end up* in between.'

Spuybroek's textile tectonics are inherently structural. It is this point of differentiation that distinguishes him from other architects working in similar ways. When he describes the structural importance of his textile tectonics he notes that:

'When you move too close to massing the technique becomes formalist, and if too close to texture it will bring you surfaces but not necessarily volume. Textile tectonics brings you exactly what it says; tectonics, yes, but tectonics with a lot of spin-off on the surface level, while the volume stays a bit behind, slightly undefined. I am closer to the roof-side of Semper's problem than to the earth-side. Frampton's Semperian reading of Utzon and Piano has had a big influence on me. I have thought a lot about how to solve the opposition of roof-enclosure and earthwork. I thought a lot

about that when working on the competition for the second Centre Pompidou in Metz (2003). In this project I took a system of portals in a linear organisation and started to split the portals and weave them into a shell. From a line-system to a surface-system. Thus developing from a hierarchical system of primary, large portals and secondary girders into a system without hierarchy, consisting in fact only of secondary elements, a shell. So, with the big, heavy portals lined up on the ground, they interlaced at the top into a light network of ribs. Like the US Congress Building, it has wings at the side and a dome in the middle – seriously. That is a very old problem in architecture, the ground plan is playing the horizontal, urbanist part, the dome is making the vertical, architectural landmark. Block and sign combined, but architecturally unresolved, just added up and quasi-knitted together – classicism can't solve problems for you, it can only create them. Our splitting and weaving technique tackled that old issue, how foundation and roof share the same continuous geometry.'

Topotectonics, Continuity and Ornament
Topotectonics, continuity and their relationship to decoration are key features of Spuybroek's unique body of work. In his

NOX, Seoul Opera House, Seoul, South Korea, 2005
Spuybroek used Gaudí's and Otto's techniques of hanging catenary curves for this project. In this case, the surface consists of a variable modulation where peaks act as megavaults, and valleys as megacolumns. The surface is made of glass triangles that are coated with a rasterised pattern making the surface vary between transparent and reflective opaque.

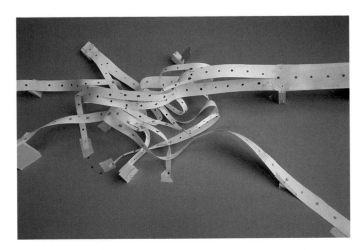

NOX, Son-O-House, Son en Breugel, the Netherlands, 2000–04
A series of paper models for the public artwork of Son-O-House was generated in the NOX office in 2001 to study the structural interlacing of paper strips.

work, topotectonics is a definitive tectonics of continuous elements, which is curious and almost paradoxical. For Frampton the continuous always leads to unhappy sculpturism, carved earthwork. Spuybroek's views on sculpturism are complex and critical. He states that:

'I want to stay far away from sculpturism, it doesn't even recognise architectural problems. I totally agree with Frampton about Gehry – though we should be for ever grateful to Gehry for stealing the technology out of high-tech offices – but it is pure formalism. Though there is a very powerful, floral logic behind Bilbao, it's not structure, it's *hardened geometry*. When you look at the steel system, all the members are at the position of the polygons. Normally you'd have substructure there and have the larger members somewhere else ... but where? So, there is no tectonics at all there, only sculpturism. What we do is very different. Textile tectonics is a *topotectonics*, meaning it's a tectonics of continuity, not of elementarism. That's exactly what makes it so difficult to read for critics. They are used, when tectonics is mentioned, to seeing joints in discontinuous surfaces. With sculpturism they are used to seeing smooth surfaces of continuous geometry. I do joints and continuous geometries! Consider my recent project, the Jeongok Prehistory Museum (2005); it's full of articulation, joints, rounded holes, spiky connections, ribs. But it is a roof that merrily connects to the ground, rejoins with the ground. To put it even stronger: it *becomes* ground. It's not dropped on the ground like Piano's Klee Museum, though I find that fascinating – I find all Piano's work fascinating, there is such a huge battle going on, rising from the ground versus flying back to earth, earth projects versus sky projects. Beautiful facades versus beautiful roofs. Now, to successfully have a roof on the ground, tectonically you have a big problem to solve, since the light structure of the roof is generally not capable of supporting floors. That's where our scale-jump comes in to help; since the textile techniques are deployed on the level of structure, not substructure – what you'd get with a shell – it can still manage floor loads.'

The Classical and the Picturesque
Spuybroek also makes a significant distinction between the classical and the picturesque in his work. These categories are for him:

'well illustrated with the case of the famous diagram of Corbusier with the four houses on a row with the classical Villa Garches and picturesque Villa La Roche. The classical starts with the whole, a box, a set of boxes, a cylinder, whatever, and then subtracts the parts. The picturesque adds up the parts to a loose whole. It's always one or the other, though in Villa Savoie you get both at the same time. I think we are solving that, the choice between whole-to-the-parts or parts-to-the-whole, between subtractive design techniques and additive design techniques. Textile techniques are *multiplicatory* techniques: whole and parts interact, send information back and forth. It's solved because of continuity, there is communication all the way through. If parts want to bulge, stick out, articulate, they can, but are corrected by a loose whole since you never get corners. That's the rule: no corners, though sharp creases and tearings are allowed since it is all material.

'For the Jeongok Prehistory Museum we manage everything with curvature. It starts with one bay at the top of the hill and it then runs down and develops into three bays, not separated but as three convex zones with two concave ones in between; then, down the hill, to where the section fully merges with the ground as a wide span to function as an entry hall. Normally you would have to add up these typologies – single bay, triple bay and hall – into a composite volume; now they are all transitory states of a single volume.'

The force of Spuybroek's developments on Semperian textile tectonics and their role in the variation and generation of volume, structure, surface and fenestration and the way in which they drive everything in a project is exemplified in NOX's Jeongkok Prehistory Museum. He is adamant that 'Semper's concept of textile drives everything'. Which is why he asserts, in conclusion, that:

'I don't need ornament. All minimalists nowadays have moved to ornament, we don't need to. With me ornament carries the load. I don't believe Semper is the theoretician of ornate surfaces, I think he is the theoretician of articulation, of making and elaborating, and there structure and ornament can never be opposed.' ◭

Note
1. 'The idea of a system of material units whose attributes are pliability, suppleness and toughness came about for the following reasons: 1. to string and to bind; 2. to cover, to protect, and to enclose.' Gottfried Semper, *Style in the Technical and Tectonic Arts*; *Or, Practical Aesthetics*, Harry Mallgrave, Los Angeles: Getty Research Institute, 2004, p 113.

Thomas More Council Estate, London: A re-Fabricated Picturesque Landscape

Charlie de Bono

Fabric and textiles have a pervasive application in the domestic setting. The way we clothe ourselves, and the use of fabrics and upholstery in the home, has always signalled the way we see ourselves, and the way we want to be seen, indicating our role in society. This idea of role is pertinent in both social interaction and buildings, and a correlation can be drawn between the two. There is something of the actor in us all – changing our clothing to suit the occasion – and perhaps buildings can and should respond similarly. We tailor our clothes to our mood, the weather or the occasion, so perhaps buildings can respond quicker and more ebulliently? How can a building endlessly modify like an actor not just its costume, but imperceptibly change its internal character according to its latest role?

A theatrical metaphor resonates the concept, but in the project featured here perhaps the principles were closer to amateur dramatics. In the same way that in this idiom there is a desire to 'make do and mend', in the prototyping process here charity shops were a more important material source than the builders' merchant. The Victorian council estate was adapted to perform in a sustainable manner, transforming its environment into a picturesque agrarian landscape. The aim was to provide a hypothetical model for the reconfiguration of existing urban housing stock, leading to a more responsible, self-reliant as well as ornamenal domestic life. The estate essentially reclothes itself. The proposal involved the tenants developing experimental methods of recycling their domestic waste (human sewage and organic kitchen) to propagate a bucolic landscape vision.

The Wilderness Gardens provide picturesque elements on the periphery of the landscape that recycle the 'humanure', and were created from domestic fabrics including curtains, blankets, dishcloths and the tenants' old clothes. Here, the humble sewing machine becomes a prime construction tool, and traditional tailoring and upholstery skills suddenly become fundamental construction techniques. The materials are predominantly domestic, where possible recycled or cheap DIY products, and the methods of construction are within the tenants' means.

The Edge of the Wilderness is a threshold membrane comprising a cable-net that supports a series of interwoven fabric cones that taper down five floors. As the compost accumulates, the structure flexes, reshapes and stiffens as the girdles are tightened around the weaves. A heady mix of sweetly scented flowers is interplanted within the fabrication, compensating for the composting odour. Underneath, a dark undercroft space is lit only by shafts of natural daylight falling through the gaps in the weave and against the rugged soaring walls of the building. ⚫

Charlie de Bono

The Big Air World: From 'Cotton' to 'Air'

Dr VA Watson

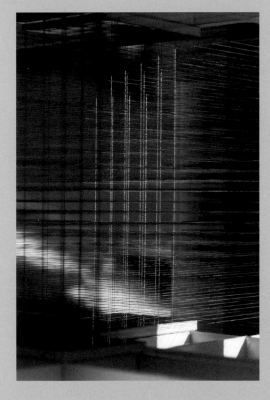

Initially, in 2003, a fascination for the grids locked into the architecture of Mies van der Rohe led to the manufacture of a three-dimensional grid, conceived as a 1/500 model of his design for the Lake Shore Drive apartments, Chicago (1951). The aim was to produce an image of the way Miesian architecture *feels*, to represent the sensation of embodied weightlessness.

The model was made as a pale-blue lattice structure of embroidery thread, sewn into a foam-board support. Gazing into it arouses curious sensations, a feeling of being drawn inside and at the same time losing one's habitual grasp of distance and scale.

Adherence to the Miesian model is not strictly necessary for the production of sensational effects: the formation of the grid relates to the structure of the visual field – the eye of the observer, ambient light, size, cadence and framing of the grid.

A further and highly significant factor affecting the formation of the grid is the introduction of a variety of colours among the constitutive threads. The multicolour grid appears more voluminous, even if in fact it has been made with no significant material increase than that of the monochrome.

The increased optical density must be understood either as an immaterial property of the grid or as a property of the material that falls between the individual threads, ie of the air. Being unsure if the sensation of voluminous colour that resonates throughout the grid is truly immaterial, we have opted for the latter and at the moment name the phenomenon under investigation 'Air'. ⧈

Dr VA Watson

Camouflage as Aesthetic Sustainability

A textile approach to architecture offers unique opportunities to explore a structure's surface and texture. Through a discussion of the history of the technique of camouflage and her own projects with Design Research and Development (DR_D), **Dagmar Richter** demonstrates the potential for surface enrichment to exceed mere ornament or patterning. A 'performative texture', camouflage interacts with its context mimicking the natural and effectively disguising whatever it covers. With a now long military association, camouflage also provides anything but a neutral background for its cover.

Design, Research and Development (DR_D) was established in three different parts of the world[1] to rethink methods of architectural design within a new digital and cultural paradigm, made possible by ever more sophisticated computer technologies. The focus of the initiative's research and experimentation is performing surfaces. Thus the concept of surface as structure and primary experiential mass – an armed surface – has become the driving force behind its architectural design practice.[2] Since 2002, DR_D has become, too, increasingly obsessed with disguise and camouflage, and through this has had the opportunity to explore an object's surface and texture in a quest for a dual interpretation of it as a natural phenomenon.

Recently, camouflage has dominated the world of fashion, which appropriated it from the design branding that identified it with the military. Fashion's attempts to subvert authority have returned the abstract representation of the natural to urban architecture.

Below is an outline of the history of camouflage and of how its origins in textiles and architecture interweave with high art and mass culture. There is much to be learned from the techniques of camouflage, since it experimented with the traditional architectural ornament as a performative texture where its effect has been closely studied for more than a hundred years.

The Ornament in Architecture
When Adolf Loos[3] questioned the material presence of architectural space in his famous book *Ornament and Crime*,[4] he echoed his father figure Gottfried Semper who had written his massive treatise, *Style in the Technical and Tectonic Arts: Or, Practical Aesthetics*, some 40 years earlier.[5] In tracing the origins of classical architecture to techniques of knotting, fabricating

and plant weaving, Semper postulated that a woven or knotted surface, providing shade and delineating space and ownership, constituted the basis from which the mythical conception of architecture should have emerged.[6] Semper's argument repeatedly challenged the status quo by advancing architecture capable of operating on the surface where a new world of references was possible. The modern taboo, namely the relationship of architecture's basic mass and construction to its superfluous ornamentation, has constituted a field of unease among practitioners ever since.

Camouflage as daywear today.

DR_D Lab (Art Academy Stuttgart), Domin(f)o House, 2002–03.

DR_D Studio (Berlin), The history of architecture in four pictograms
Olmsted's stable block, Tschumi's Parc de la Villette, OMA's Downsview Park and DR_D's City=Park project.

From Semper, who questioned architecture's postulated origins by re-establishing the ornamented surface as its primary precedent, to Loos who then redefined the ornamented surface as a crime, the ornament has moved constantly on our architectural radar screens, oscillating in and out of focus, and has now once again found a steady foothold in contemporary practice. The former Modernist constructive wall, as for example the carefully positioned walls at the Barcelona Pavilion by Mies van der Rohe, is being re-evaluated with the help of new technical possibilities in what becomes an endeavour to collapse our cherished taboo of structure versus ornament into a single, highly textured performative surface with the capacity to satisfy all programmatic parameters simultaneously.

The Textured Enclosure: An Architectural Medium from Diverse Cultures

To set this outline in a more political context: from 1851 Semper began to see architecture in a more comparative light, describing the development of architectural origins with reference to the construction techniques of many different cultures. He gave illustrated examples of numerous architectural surfaces, starting with simple, everyday structures and going on to include festive and representational built work by cultures which previously had been considered either too irrelevant or too primitive to act as precedents, thus opening up a whole new world of references beyond Western classicism.[7] Today, fascination with the textile origin of architecture reflects renewed interest in the existence of architecture as a global cultural phenomenon. The ornament as a textured and patterned conceptual basis and traditional element of Islamic cultural presentation, the origns of China's highly textured garden and rock structures, and the structure and texture of plants – all are now recognised as contributing to an enhanced appreciation of the form and function of adornment, and all are studied with the aim of finding once again more diverse precedents that have global value.

Ornament, Photography and Camouflage

Soon after Semper, the architectural surface became the subject of flat and animated image production through the invention of photography and film.[8] With the help of the airship, aeroplane and satellite, the angle of view towards the world has shifted from the interior and exterior perspective to the axonometric, to aerial photography and satellite imagery relayed from afar. The art of photography and its use by the military intersected with Modern artists and architects in a most intriguing way at the beginning of the 20th century. During the First World War, aerial photography began to have a measurable impact, as the armies of Europe and the US needed to reassess their strategies in the light of this novel technology which made them so much more vulnerable to their enemies. Suddenly, military targets could be reconnoitred from above by pilots able to locate objects and units with precision and in relative safety. The military asked artists and architects to analyse the images of the objects photographed. To protect structures on the ground, there was an urgent need to find, through the invention of novel forms of ornamentation, surface treatments that had the effect of blurring these objects as well as blending and morphing them into the extreme textured background of their locations. The technique of camouflage was studied intensively[9] for its effect on its audience, the pilot whose speed of flight prevented detailed scrutiny of a single event or object. In fact, this pilot's behaviour mirrored that of the public of today, immersed in fast and fleeting images that constitute a concentrated distraction with massive Attention Deficit Disorder (ADD), as Helen Furjan has described.[10] Many Modern European and American artists and architects were hired to dissolve a given collection of images into the background to the point of erasure.[11] Their question, 'How is it that we see an object?', was directly linked to the question 'How can we prevent an object from being seen?'.

The visual misreading of an object by the military revisits our dilemma of the natural versus the artificial, the virtual versus the real, multiples versus singularities just as the flat in camouflage mimics the extreme texture of natural environments. Simultaneously, the masses of soldiers operating on the ground moved conceptually into the realm of art, specifically that of Modern art, that was experienced in an immersive form. The unpredictable patterns of light and shadow cast from the elaborate nettings with leaf-like ornamentation in the wind, the bold graphic images of their ships, the abstract, moving paintings in the form of tanks and cannons opened the soldiers' eyes to a hitherto unexplored world of art and design. With the help of this new audience those same masters of camouflage, among them Abbot Thayer, Jacques Villon, Oskar Schlemmer, Edward Wadsworth, Arshile Gorky, Grant Wood, László Moholy-Nagy and Ellsworth Kelly, became respected, established Modern artists after the war.

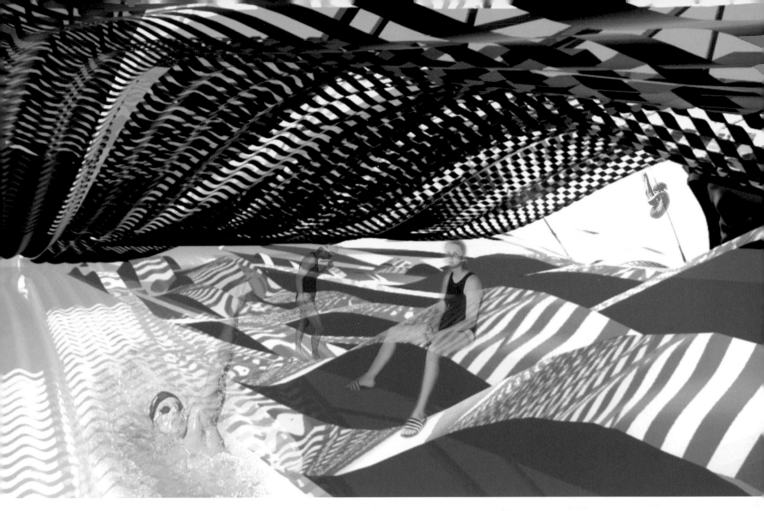

DR_D Studio (Santa Monica), The Wave, 2000–02
The design aims to blend the existing building into the existing landscape via its additions.

Today, camouflage is an ubiquitous textile surface in times of peace at fashion shows and is used intensively as a kind of branding for anything to be understood as military. As Bush stands in front of CNN cameras in Iraq in his traditional Vietnam camouflage outfit mimicking a life in the jungle, camouflage's new brand identity can be observed, a brand no longer used to disguise the president from the viewer – rather, the reverse. Once again, camouflage reflects contemporary culture, here studied and employed by specialists who manipulate its marketing potential for a media-savvy society.

Hardy Blechman's thoroughly researched and informative book *DPM*,[12] the author himself the creator of the Maharishi fashion label, helped the DR_D studio move in some measure towards new fields of experimentation in architecture, namely to investigate new possibilities embedded in the architectural surface, its texture and its blurring effect for a user heavily distracted by the visual barrage of modern life. As the academic world moved quietly from engagement with the approach of Peter Eisenman and Daniel Libeskind towards Herzog & de Meuron, a progression from a discursive and text-oriented architecture to one that is hoping to produce an effect so powerfully experiential that it results in an affect, a new cultural paradigm emerged. In the words of Marc Angelil and Sarah Graham: 'Intrinsic is the tendency to transgress

DR_D Lab (Art Academy Stuttgart), Domin(f)o House, 2002–03
In this vertical prototype, the surface redefines the entire deep structure of the building and offers, through its highly textured new surface, a green facade, a habitat for birds as well as extra shading. Further development was by the DR_D Studio (Berlin).

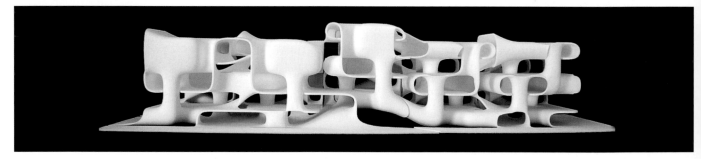

Through a digital transformation process the former surface of the original structure reorganises the entire depth, and through its newly textured surface redefines plan and section alike.

physical perimeters or to blur contour lines, a strategy capable of serving diverging tasks'.[13] DR_D hopes to contribute to this recent search for an architectural performance that fulfils these criteria. To this end, its recent work has moved the ornament-as-adornedment away from the surface of the facade into the heart of the building.

To see the construction of architecture as the outcome of a cumulative process that is repetitive and rhythmic, starts to move the architectural object from a figurative, distinctive effect towards its function as the sum, ie the accumulation, of experiential qualities. DR_D's new techniques try to obtain an unfocused quality by visually blurring the object into the background. It is hoped that this technique will contribute to a more sustainable built environment, capable of halting the frenzy of novel production and immediate demolition, by rejecting/preventing the object being read as novel or contemporary and so deemed to be outdated even before it is completed.

In 1993, DR_D attempted for the first time to morph the design of a building proposal into the background as part of the design submission for the National Library in Copenhagen, Denmark.[14] Our team was barely aware of our sudden unease at the prospect of inserting a monumental object into the fabric of this historic city when we chose to experiment instead with a natural technique of blending in order to regenerate Copenhagen's extraordinary waterfront: a technique we called 'the art of copy'. From then on camouflage helped reformulate an architectural strategy that used textured surfaces and their constructive properties to find new territories for contemporary spatial production. The studio experimented with the textural and graphic quality of camouflage by reassigning depth into new independent, woven, labyrinthian and localised spaces in order to promote a spatial model that blurs spatial hierarchies and visual distinction. In DR_D's project proposal The Wave, for a new water park around an existing sports hall in Aalborg, Denmark, for example, camouflage was explored as a technique for morphing the existing monumental sports hall and its proposed additions into the existing landscape through several layers of textured surfaces.

Camouflage's strategy of flattening the extreme texture of the object's natural context graphically on to the flat surface was used in a technique of reversal. Incorporating what was learned from the transformation of the natural texture to the

DR_D Lab (Art Academy Stuttgart), The Living Museum: Pimp My Architecture, 2005
Interior perspective of an exhibition showroom. Through its programmed lighting the extreme texture of the structural surface creates atmospheres between mystery and blinding dazzle.
(Professor Dagmar Richter and Research Director Jonas Luther. Project designers Eva Greiner, Lukasz Ledinsky and Sascha Seidel.)

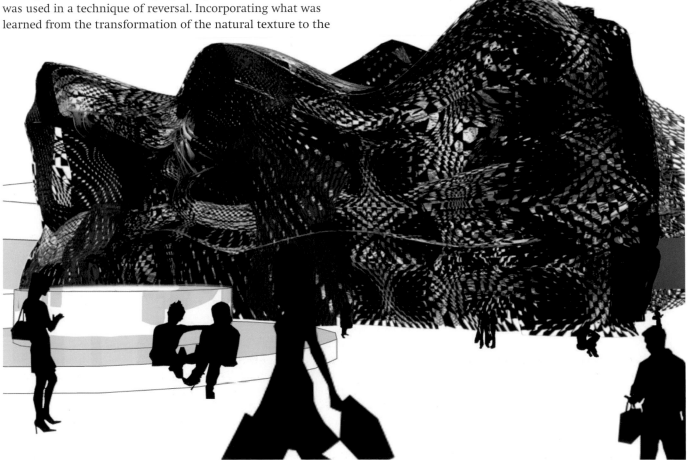

Seen from Alexanderplatz in Berlin at light-up time, through highly textured surfaces, the Living Museum not only brings a new urban depth to the Alexanderplatz, but additionally blends into the highly branded surroundings as a mysterious background.

artificial flat, the reversal regained the textured quality of the artificial by employing this tried and tested process. For the first set of experiments, Le Corbusier's Dom-Ino House was used as a modern prototype for housing production. Today's housing needs were identified and the issue examined of how surfaces could be reformulated utilising novel technologies to improve their performance for a new prototype, the Dom-in(f)o house. Simultaneously, DR_D started to build up a library of prototypical surface constructions in order to provide an expanded vocabulary of known properties and textures with the help of digital design and rapid prototyping.

In a further experiment, the prominent facade of a large department store at Berlin Alexanderplatz was examined. At the time, this facade was undergoing a face-lift in the spirit of new urbanism that had the effect of erasing one of the last true socialist, complexly folded metal curtains by the Hungarian architects Simon and Fokvari. Three research teams from the DR_D Lab at the Art Academy in Stuttgart assessed various possibilities for rewrapping the department store with a highly textured surface that would blur the boundaries of the building in this prominent city context, confront anew its relationship to the interior of the department store and reconsider its programmatic definition as display. The new proposal for a museum of living arts pitted traditional consumerist store display against the wisdom of educational museum display design to provide space for the sale and production of prototype clothing and accessories. The project shown here, called Pimp My Architecture, investigates current TV culture and its celebration of 'bling'. Several TV series act as reference points in that they overtly blur distinctions and traditional definitions of high and low culture by using 'pimp' as a technique of upgrading otherwise rather unappealing objects of consumer culture. From this seemingly unpromising material, dazzling effects are created through this design of an adaptive atmosphere that supports times of exuberant celebration as well as quiet down- and work-time using surfaces of extreme texture. Through the application of different levels of internal reflective gold surfaces set against nonreflective exterior surfacing, a new skin of exuberant interiority was created. The team's highly textured surface supported an array of different atmospheres by means of surface texturing, coating and lighting techniques.

Finding an alternative to the architectural object representing progress and criticality in the form of *architecture parlante*, or the classicist approach, is the main aim of DR_D's practice. In the projects shown here, various natural and military techniques have been appropriated. What is attempted is to leave the building-as-object in an undecided state, by merging it into the background through extreme textural morphing and by eradicating the object's line of delineation, blurring inside and outside, object and context, to enable the opening up of further possibilities of appropriation and engagement. It is hoped this will allow for more vivid responses that are not triggered solely by passive

consumption of a given sensationalist environment, but rather by breaking down the dichotomy between the natural and the artificial to stimulate a contemplative delight embedded in the complexity of textile surfaces. ⌂

Notes

1. DR_D Studio, 2640 Highland Ave, Santa Monica, CA 90405; DR_D Lab, Department of Architecture and Urban Design, UCLA (2002–05 at the Art Academy Stuttgart); DR_D Office, Rhinowerstrasse 10, 10437 Berlin, Germany.
2. For examples of recent work by DR_D, see Dagmar Richter, *XYZ: The Architecture of Dagmar Richter*, Princeton Architectural Press (Princeton, NJ), 2001, and Armed Surfaces, Black Dog Publishing (London), 2003.
3. See Adolf Loos, *Ornament and Crime: Selected Essays*, Ariadne Press (Riverside, CA), 1998.
4. Ibid.
5. Gottfried Semper, *Style in the Technical and Tectonic Arts; Or, Practical Aeshetics*, Getty Research Institute Publications (Los Angeles), 2004.
6. 'Scaffolds that served to hold, secure, or support this spatial enclosure had nothing directly to do with *space* or the *division of space*. They were foreign to the original architectural idea and were never form-determining elements to start with … Whether the gradual development of these inventions occurred in this order or not matters little to us here, for it is certain that a kind of crude weaving began with the pen, as a means of dividing the "home" the *inner life* from the *outer life*, as a formal construct of the spatial idea. It preceded the simple wall made from stone or another material.' In Semper, op cit, pp 248ff.
7. 'The great Exhibition of 1851 in London provided us with much material on the question at hand. Of particular importance were the textile products of primitive and domesticated peoples and architectural fittings of these peoples. The art of weaving and the associated arts of dyeing and ornamentation were represented from their earliest beginnings to the point of their greatest refinement. One had the opportunity to see how among nearly all these peoples those arts made early rapid progress and then stagnated, possibly for millennia. One would think that this lull in progress in the technical arts must have coincided with a hardening of civilizations into a certain form, which at times found expressions in architecture and monumental art. Architectural expression must then have corresponded to the state of the technical arts (and in particular to textiles, the mother of all arts) at this fateful moment in the life of a people and must have reflected this state in its symbolic language of form.' In Semper, op cit.
8. Marc Wigley has studied intensively this historic transformation and his writings on the subject provide an ample resource.
9. In 1909, the American artist Abbot Thayer wrote *Laws of Disguise: Concealing Coloration in the Animal Kingdom*.
10. 'The contemporary explosion of digital media has generated a twofold erosion of Guy Debord's culture of spectacle; an "overexposure" to the flows of information and images that creates a loss of registration (a kind of digital ADD) and a shift away from spectatorship toward immersion and interaction, which breaks down the authority of the viewing subject and engages other senses – an experiential understanding of space concerned with atmosphere and effect … distraction is created by flooding the visual field with information, demanding, as a result, not a hyperconcentration, but an absorption that pushes perception to its limits: a distracted concentration, or a concentrated distraction.' Helen Furjan, 'Atmosphere', in S Lavin and H Furnan (eds), *Crib Sheets: Notes on Contemporary Architectural Conversation*, Monacelli Press (New York), 2005, p 71.
11. Three techniques were widely employed: 1) Blending it into the background (the chameleon technique); 2) Destroying its figure by creating erratic and strong graphic patterns that allow the figure to be erased (the zebra technique); 3) Making it look like something else (the hoverfly technique).
12. Hardy Blechman, *DPM Disruptive Pattern Material, An Encyclopaedia of Camouflage: Nature-Military-Culture*, DPM Ltd (London), 2004.
13. Marc Angelil and Sarah Graham, 'Surface', in S Lavin and H Furjan, op cit, p 64.
14. See Dagmar Richter, 'The Art of Copy', *XYZ: The Architecture of Dagmar Richter*, op cit, p 96.

The Great Veil of the Central Axis

Massimiliano Fuksas

The design of the New Trade Fair Milan (2005) chooses to make the longitudinal connection axis its main generator, becoming a spine that gives structure to the entire complex. This space, the 'central axis', represents the place of activities, the centre of information, the place of crossing and at the same time of being. These concepts are developed through the positioning of a series of buildings alongside the main axis, having connections at level 0,00 and at footbridge level + 6.50.

The buildings host various functions: restaurants, meeting rooms, office spaces and receptions to connect the exhibition halls. Those along the central axis are suspended above diversely treated landscaped areas: water, green areas and concrete. The flanking stainless-steel and glass facades of the exhibition halls become the scenography. Above the whole of the space extends the vast roof covering – an undulating lightweight structure like a veil.

With a surface area exceeding 46,000 square metres (495,140 square feet), the veil is bordered by the pavilion facade-line for the entire length of the central axis. Constituted from a reticular rhomboidal mesh structure in prefinished steel profiles, it is connected via spherical nodes and covered with laminated glass fixed through plates to the profiles below. The structural mesh utilises modules of 2.7 x 2.25 metres (8.9 x 7.4 feet) to obtain one constant width along the central axis of 31.57 metres (103.57 feet), and on the east and the west entrances a width of 40.59 metres (133.17 feet). Its height varies from +16 metres (52 feet) to around +23 metres (75 feet). The mesh structure includes more than 32,000 nodes, giving 38,929 rhomboid frames. The form of the veil is derived from constant altimetric variations, just as are found in the natural landscape – for example, 'craters', 'waves', 'dunes' and 'hills'. As a natural landscape the shape is never repetitive, giving visitors an animating, continuously varying perspective. ᗝ

Massimiliano Fuksas

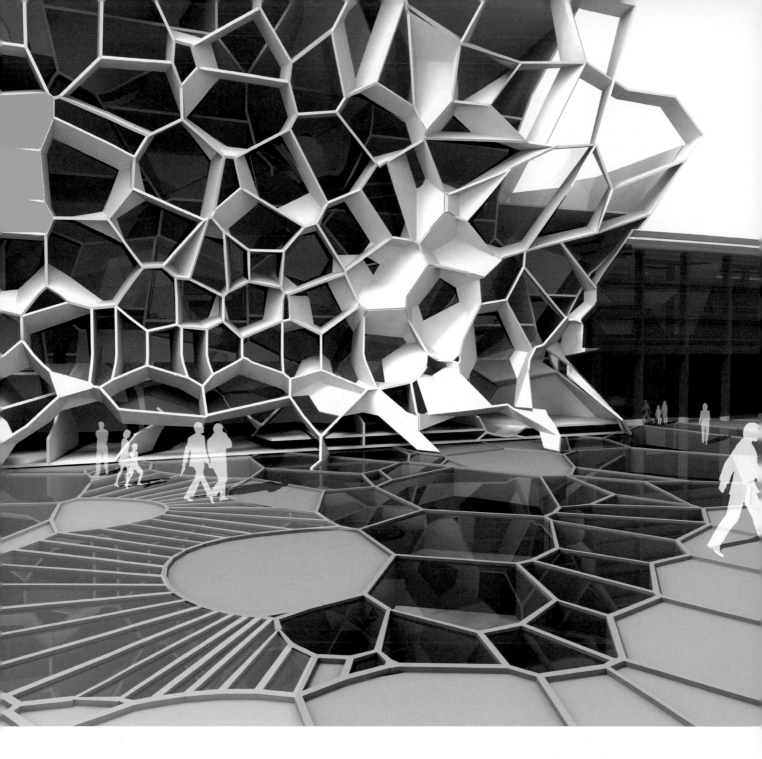

Parametric Matter

The assimilation of digital techniques in production and manufacturing has enabled innovative explorations into nonstandard material organisation. **Yusuke Obuchi**, **Theodore Spyropoulos** and **Tom Verebes** of the Design Research Lab (DRL) at the Architectural Association (AA) describe how an interest in a textiles approach has developed out of a preoccupation with the interrelationship between material and computational design methods. They describe three projects that aspire to embed forms of material intelligence into architectural space.

The material paradigm presented here is one of the continual transformation of deep three-dimensional textures and patterns via the distribution of a serial, iterative spatial logic, aggregating to form continuous yet discrete material organisations. New digital design, production and manufacturing procedures enable the possibilities to create forms of materialisation beyond the assembly of predefined components, causing nonuniform yet continuously differentiated local articulation and expression within an identifiable larger organisation. These material systems share properties with the ways in which textiles are grown out of aggregating smaller operations to achieve larger, more coherent material organisations.

In the last decade, the Architectural Association Design Research Lab (DRL)[1] has continually explored the potentials of today's highly distributed, digital design networks and tools, as well as the innovative forms of materialisation emerging within this electronic realm of digital design disciplines. One of its primary areas of research is the interrelationship between material and computational design methods, investigating the potential to generate material organisations with active rather than inert behaviours. Its design processes seek to bridge the gap between digital procedures and their relation to the assembly of physical material components, using advanced scripting and techniques to develop complex material systems that are informed and tested through digital and material performance simulations. The relation of advanced computational design procedures to their implementation and materialisation as projects lies in the strategy to deploy continuously transforming dynamic patterns and textures in three-dimensional parametrically controlled material constructions. The three DRL projects documented here deploy a range of computational techniques that aim to embed new forms of material intelligence into architectural space.

Algorithmic Porous Patterns
The Netlab design research work of the G_nome team of the DRL exemplifies how algorithms can be applied parametrically in the formation of design systems in relation to specific contingent criteria. Recursive computational design procedures allow for feedback, adjustment and optimisation of specific organisational conditions of a project brief. The Voronoi diagramming tool is the primary design tool in this project, benefiting from its capacity to output continuous yet discrete cellular spaces, blending walls, floors and structure as a continuous and unifying volumetric material fabric.

Using a series of expressions and scripts to compute the Voronoi diagram in three dimensions, parametric design variation of the material patterns and porosities is achieved

according to a set of criteria related to each design system. Sets of user, programmatic, contextual and environmental information are embedded as the evaluation criteria in the organisation of the building, allowing each script to articulate highly differentiated material effects in each system. These dynamic parameters differentiate the patterning of porosity of the building's lattice structure, interior partitions, screens and facade systems. Such design systems act as filters and channels to manage the flow of people, the dynamic performance of activities, and the permeation of filtered light and views throughout the hard material fabric of the building.

Topological Urban Fabric
Another DRL project, Hybrid Species, by the YME team, rethinks the stratified office building as a descendant of the Maison Dom-Ino model of spatial organisation and industrial

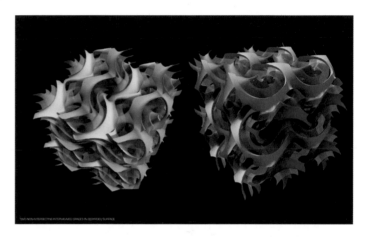

Differentiation of minimal-level surfaces using Mathematica software. The recursive structure of this serial approach to formal differentiation allows the designer to interact with the modelling environment, importing feedback to adjust the local surface conditions of the cells, while reconfiguring the global organisation and maintaining its overall coherence.

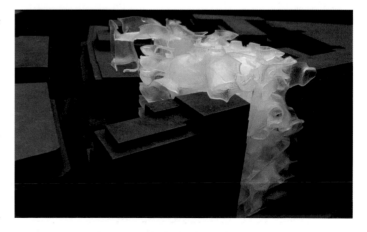

G_nome team (Ibraheem Ammash, Jimena Araiza, Maria Loreto Flores and Ahmad Sukkar), Netlab, Tom Verebes studio, DRL, 2004–06
Opposite: View of exterior indicating urban plaza and building threshold systems, designed with differentiating scripts of the Voronoi algorithm to achieve geometrical output specific to the criteria of each design system.

YME team (Yevgehniy Beylkin, Elif Erdine and Margarita Valova), Hybrid Species, Brett Steele studio, DRL, 2004–06
3-D print model of triply periodic minimal-level surfaces inset into the urban context. The dense set of recursive cells and strata of matter of the proposal are contrasted to the Cartesian geometry and dense opacity of the existing buildings.

Fabric Architecture and Flexible Design

Robert Kronenburg is one of the leading advocates of portable and flexible architecture. Over the last decade he has written substantial books and curated major international shows on the subject. Here he highlights how recent innovations in material and digital techniques have facilitated the onset of a new type of fabric architecture that is able to house increasingly larger and culturally more significant facilities. Outlining the most pertinent technological developments in the field, he also provides a comprehensive account of some of the most important projects.

Fabric architecture has an organic, sinuous, delicate form that is indicative of elegant and ambitious modern building. Recent innovations in materials and techniques have dramatically expanded its potential into much larger, high-profile, culturally important architecture projects. Advanced tensile fabrics that are flexible, strong and environmentally stable have led to more sophisticated computer-aided design methods resulting in efficient structures that can enclose large spaces with low building mass. Twin-layer membranes can also make these more environmentally efficient, and a wide range of opacity and surface treatments can create various interior ambiences.

Though there is now a wide range of commercially available membrane mobile buildings, this form of construction is still being explored for dedicated building designs that push its capabilities further. Tensile fabric structures use struts and cables for support and bracing, and many evocative and elegant shapes can be created in this way. Low-pressure pneumatic structures can be column free if based on air-supported principles where a relatively higher internal air pressure keeps the roof aloft. High-pressure air columns, beams and walls can be erected very quickly.

Fabric structures also have specific attributes that enable them to provide solutions to difficult building problems that require innovative and flexible approaches. They are particularly valuable in the creation of adaptable, mobile and interactive building environments, and in the most recent projects the availability of new and developing technologies has led to the introduction of interactive architectural strategies whereby responsive building environments are the goal.[1]

FTL Design and Engineering Studio has created many tensile fabric buildings that fulfil a wide range of functions, from retail development to convention halls and performance buildings. One of its most important structures is the Carlos Moseley Music Pavilion, first commissioned in 1991. Still in regular use each year, it was made for a series of outdoor classical music performances in New York's parks. The concept was to create a structure that could provide facilities to make concert-hall-quality performances available externally to a large audience. It consists of a 21-metre (69-foot) high tripod structure built on to five standard flatbed trucks. This supports a PVDF Teflon-coated polyester fabric membrane that provides a dramatic backdrop for performances, particularly when lit at night. More importantly, it also provides a semirigid rain cover and sound reflector to acoustically project the music towards the audience. Concert hall acoustics are replicated by a sophisticated Bose sound system that builds in reverberation time that would normally only be heard indoors.

FTL's Machine Tent for the Harley-Davidson Travelling Tour (2002) is an exhibition building that commemorates the motorcycle manufacturer's 100th anniversary. Externally, it is reminiscent of a conventional single-pole tent form. However, it actually has a total of seven masts – a primary one in the centre and six secondary ones to form a hexagon on plan. Though the structure is 50 metres (164 feet) in diameter, it can be erected without extra equipment using winches wired within the masts to haul up the elevated components. The masts are also used to carry lighting and communications equipment associated with the exhibition. An important feature of the building was that it had to meet the codes of all the countries it would travel to, including Australia, Canada, Mexico and Japan, an issue that adds to the complexity of designing internationally mobile buildings.[2]

The largest tented structure in the world is the Valhalla system designed by Rudi Enos and operated by Gearhouse Structures in the UK. It is a modular building that can be

KieranTimberlake Associates, SmartWrap building, New York, 2003
A prototype exhibition structure, the building was assembled at the Cooper-Hewitt Museum to promote the potential of the thin-skin interactive SmartWrap building membrane.

Inflate, Unipart Structure, UK, 2004
The exhibition structure is a hybrid utilising a slender metal truss to support two inflatable truncated cones.

Inflate, Big M, UK, 2005
This economic yet effective exhibition structure uses familiar low-level 'bouncy castle' technology.

heat. A change from liquid to solid results in a release of heat, and a change from solid to liquid results in absorption of heat. PCMs are utilised to absorb climactic heat when the temperature is high and release it when the temperature drops. Lighting and information display is implemented by an organic, light-emitting diode display (OLED). OLEDs are based on organic molecules that emit light when electric current is applied, and are either made in polymer form or small molecules that can be deposited directly on to the polymer substrate. They have lower energy use, better resolution, are thinner and flexible in comparison to current flatscreen displays. Power supply is provided using innovative organic photovoltaics that convert light (photons) into a steady stream of electricity (electrons) transferred to a coating of Buckminsterfullerene (C60) in order to sustain the OLED system. These layers are transferred to the SmartWrap substrate using a continuous roll-printing system called Deposition printing that is similar to inkjet printing. Different layers of SmartWrap can also be laminated together in a rapid automated system for factory production.

Festo KG, Airquarium, Germany, 2001
An air-supported mobile exhibition building, the Airquarium uses a water-filled torus for stability. The remarkable translucency of the dome is made possible by the innovative Vitroflex membrane.

Festo KG, Airtecture Hall, Germany, 1999
Many different technologies are tested in this product of blue-sky research.

Though all of the technology used in SmartWrap is proven, its transition to full manufacturing capability is still under way. However, a prototype building for the Cooper-Hewitt Museum in New York (2003) is an exemplar of the potential of the material, and also incorporates an exhibition showing the principles behind its design and manufacture. The SmartWrap created for the pavilion has a thermal transmittance value that is comparable to a conventional concrete block and brick cavity wall with a 50-millimetre (2-inch) airspace and 50-millimetre (2-inch) expanded polystyrene insulation, though with just 1/100th weight.

Interactive design is one manifestation of the implementation of developing technologies that are making possible new constructional and operational strategies that are improvements on existing methods. The potential of thin fabric- and membrane-based structure and cladding systems that fulfil all the environmental tasks of conventional built-up construction could lead to an unprecedented shift in the way buildings are designed. The result would be a fabric-based architecture that requires much lighter supporting structures with consequent savings in materials and erection costs. It could also mean buildings that are more independent of external services, saving on infrastructure, but also on central power generation. These factors have benefits in terms of efficiency, sustainability and the environment. However, they could also help develop a more flexible, comfortable and responsive relationship for people with the architecture they use.

Fabric architecture has inherent advantages in terms of flexibility for both large- and small-scale projects, either for mobility, such as the Airtecture Hall, or for adaptation, as with SmartWrap. The drive towards more flexible buildings and environments is an important part of future architectural development – fabrics will undoubtedly play a large part in this future. ⌂

Notes
1. This essay previews some ideas from the author's book *Flexible: Architecture That Responds to Change*, Laurence King (London), 2007.
2. For a detailed examination of FTL's tensile projects see Chapter 12 of the author's book *Portable Architecture* (3rd edition), Architectural Press (Oxford), 2003.
3. One of Inflate's simplest 'building' structures is Office in a Bucket, an inflatable partition system that arrives in a bucket no bigger than an office wastebasket. It creates a defined, private meeting space that can be stored in a very small space when it is not in use. See Nick Crosbie, *I'll Keep Thinking*, Black Dog Publishing (London and New York), 2003.
4. For a detailed examination of Festo's building projects see Chapter 4 of *Portable Architecture*, op cit.
5. Other designers are finding uses for Festo technology: Kas Oosterhuis has developed a concept using the Fluidic Muscle to create an Adaptive Facade (2003), an inflatable sunshade device that is more economic in material and maintenance costs, but also more interactive and dynamic in operation.
6. See S Kieran and J Timberlake, *Refabricating Architecture: How Manufacturing Methodologies are Poised to Transform Building Construction*, McGraw Hill (Higher Education) (New York), 2004.

Architextiles

Royal College of Art Departments of Architecture and Textiles

Textiles no longer need or deserve to be considered solely as a decorative addition to a building. Recent developments in materials have broadened the definition of textiles and of the textile designer. The diversity of new materials extends beyond yarn and fibre, and emerging technologies have added to the processes employed in practice. The new possibilities for combinations of materials offer endless scope for creating new solutions for aesthetic and functional problems. New materials, technologies and manufacturing processes are forcing textile designers to move into other areas and the discipline is expanding, fragmenting and becoming more specialised and challenging.

Just as the definition of textiles as materials has significantly moved on from traditional understanding, the identity of the textile designer has also shifted away from known parameters. The understanding and knowledge of the behavioural, aesthetic, sensory and emotional properties of a number of existing and new materials are now being explored through increasingly detailed and complex, practical processes and experiments by a new breed of research-based textile designers. The importance of sustained, rigorous and imaginative physical engagement with the 'stuff' cannot be overemphasised in terms of learning and innovation. The textile designer will always have at heart an intimate and tacit knowledge of materials and their properties including colour, surface qualities, pattern, structure, behaviour and effect under fluid and complex conditions. Though many of the material experiments carried out by the textile designer are on a domestic scale, the creative possibilities behind them has potential way beyond the limitations of these immediate dimensions. The designer can no longer exist in isolation and depends on interaction with other disciplines to reach new horizons.

The growth of the applications of new textiles has resulted in the subject becoming increasingly multidisciplinary. As a response to such developments, the Architextiles project was designed and delivered by myself and Mark Garcia as a joint venture by the architecture and textiles departments at the Royal College of Art (RCA). With support from architects, engineers and textile designers, the seminars and workshops were developed to generate new forms of multidisciplinary interaction, and to apply designing, making and critical frameworks and theories to challenge the accepted concepts, boundaries and practices of each discipline. This initiative has brought together architecture and textiles design students to design hybrid, large-scale interventions. The ongoing series of work-in-progress projects proposes critical, personal design ideas that develop possible solutions to current and significant sociocultural problems. ⚙

Anne Toomey

RCA students (Joanna Kay Lewis, Anne-Laure Carruth and Laura Perryman), Knit Happens, Chatham, 2006
The project helps to build a greener urban environment by anticipating and harmonising a space with the entropic and organic processes of ruin. Using a circular knitting technique, woven carbon-fibre tubes are made with pockets for planting and with integrated watering and drainage systems. By designing the seed and plant placement and embedding these within the knitting, the natural growth of plants will take over the structure to create a living and evolving pattern across walls, over columns and around building skins.

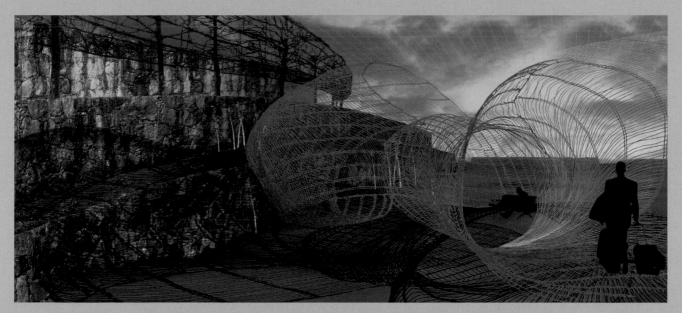

RCA students (Richard Claridge and Helen Giles), Faraday cage woven into Stansted Airport terminal landscape, 2006
The landscape of Stansted Airport's terminal building is here 'planted' with copper Faraday cages, formed by exploiting the bias of their leno-woven construction. Inside these rooms, electromagnetic fields will be controlled (known as van Eck Phreaking), enabling monitoring of terrorists and smugglers and limiting wi-fi signal 'leakage'. The vegetal forms of the structures are contained within the glass-enclosed and terraced landscape of the airport terminal buildings, creating sculptural, relaxing wi-fi-free zones.

RCA students (Sara Burns and Robert Hirschfield), Melting Pot – A knot building, City of London, 2006
Drawing inspiration from knots and knot forms, the project shows how designing architecture using a 'textile way of thinking' can enhance interaction among its users. By multiplying circulation routes and path connections, the increased possibilities for chance encounters encourage creative and complex movement patterns around the building. These increase the potential for social synergies between people from different disciplines or cultures and help to produce superior collaborations and products.

RCA students (Yuko Kanemura, Bonnie Kirkwood and Will Newton), ACOUS-Textile Auditorium, Barking, London, 2006
This project, for a concert hall next to a busy motorway in east London, utilises woven textiles (for internal partitions) and textile-moulded vacuum-formed printed plastic and polycarbonate as an acoustic double-skinned external cladding. The woven material is composed of reflective yarns of silk, steel, copper and gold. Attached to the external polycarbonate shell, this membrane forms a tensile membrane that envelops the auditorium and acts as an acoustic insulator. Windows and openings for circulation in the building are made from a devore print technique.

Anish Kapoor, Cecil Balmond and Arup AGU,
Marsyas, Tate Modern, London, 2002
View from the Turbine Hall entrance.

Woven Surface and Form

The Advanced Geometry Unit (AGU) at Arup, founded by Cecil Balmond and Charles Walker, has become synonymous with a highly mathematical, topological approach to architecture. It has, however, collaborated on some of the most exciting experimental fabric structures of recent years, including Anish Kapoor's *Marsyas* at Tate Modern and Rem Koolhaas's Cosmic Egg at the Serpentine Gallery. Here, the unit's **Tristan Simmonds**, **Martin Self** and **Daniel Bosia** describe how the AGU has progressed research into textile techniques that encompass tailored biomorphic forms alongside knot diagrams.

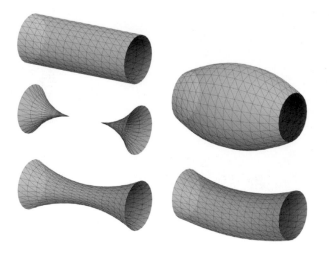

Arup AGU, Geometry research, 2002
Form-finding of a cylindrical mesh. Anticlockwise from top left: starting mesh; collapsed catenoid form resulting from equal tension in warp and weft directions; catenoid form produced using 7:1 warp to weft tension; addition of hydrostatic pressure; addition of internal pressure.

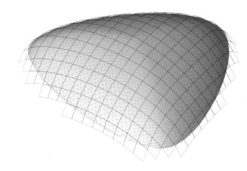

Arup AGU, Geometry research, 2005
Draping of an equal-link-length grid over an arbitrary meshed surface using ELM.

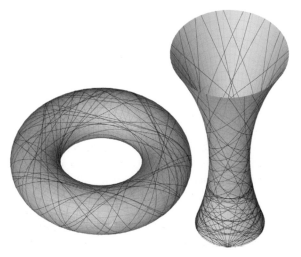

Arup AGU, Geometry research, 2005
Straight lines drawn over toroidal and catenoidal meshes show possible trajectories for structural ribbons.

Fabric structures seem to have an almost cult status among architecture students. They appear to offer highly expressive yet pure architectural and engineering solutions, they combine the oldest and newest construction materials and design techniques and they bridge the gap between the transitory and the permanent, linking architecture, fashion, performance and sculpture in what is a highly attractive mix of the aesthetic and the functional. So why do fabric structures seldom evolve past the cost-effective cladding on a stadium roof or the curious forms that keep people dry between the car park and airport terminal?

In reality large expanses of shiny white PVC- or PTFE- coated glass cloth do not always make good architecture. In practice the construction opportunities for conventional fabric structures, both geometric and material, are quite limited.

In 2002 the Advanced Geometry Unit (AGU) at Arup was founded by Vice Chairman Cecil Balmond, with a remit to research and implement new approaches to structural and architectural form. The principal areas of investigation for the AGU have been the evolution of 'conventional' form-finding techniques for application to a broader array of form and construction as well as more abstract mathematical approaches to architectural topology in general.

By starting with fabric structures and ending with the application of knot diagrams to architectural and structural topology, the following sections attempt to illustrate the technical and philosophical progression of the AGU's work in this area over the past four years.

The Nonlinear Soap-Film

The principles of physical form-finding used in 20th-century architecture have been well documented over the years, starting with Gaudí's hanging chain models in the early 1900s and culminating in the work of Frei Otto in the 1960s and 1970s, and the exhaustive research and publications of the Institute of Lightweight Structures in Stuttgart which are still a continual source of inspiration to the AGU.

The biggest revolution in form-finding, and one that is still in progress, started with the adoption of computer methods in the 1970s. Since then physical modelling has on the whole been relegated to the status of conceptual tool and, by indulging the standards of most handmade Spandex and foam-board models, it is a dying art. Computer modelling on the other hand is continuing to bring, year after year, enormous benefits and freedom to the processes of creative design, engineering and construction. It is bringing together industries as diverse as computer games, architecture and aerospace, and is coming full circle to allow the building of precise and intricate models as well as final fabrications using rapid prototyping and CNC technologies.

However, the soap-film model is far from dead. The analogy of the soap film to describe and simulate the geometry and behaviour of a membrane structure is alive and well but now living in the virtual world. Here, the soap film exists as an approximation to a smooth curving surface using a mesh of

Rem Koolhaas, Cecil Balmond and Arup AGU, Serpentine Pavilion, Hyde Park, London, 2006
View of the Cosmic Egg from behind the Serpentine Gallery.

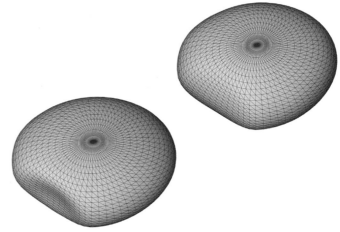

Arup AGU, Geometry research, 2002
Application of the nip-and-tuck algorithm on the 2006 Serpentine Pavilion. Before (left) and after (middle).

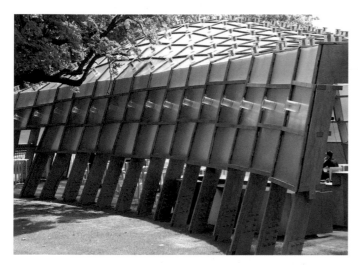

Álvaro Siza, Eduardo Souto de Moura, Cecil Balmond and Arup AGU, Serpentine Pavilion, Hyde Park, London, 2005
Left: Exterior view; Right: Interior view.

small triangular facets, each with controllable internal forces and virtual material properties. Combined with other elements that might simulate the behaviour of physical objects such as beams, cables and foundations, the system 'exists' within an environment that can simulate the structural effects of gravity, wind, snow, hydrostatic and a host of other imposed forces.

But why stick to the soap-film analogy? Lawrence Fishburne's line, 'Do you think my being faster, stronger has anything to do with my muscles in this place?' in *The Matrix* neatly conveys that a computer simulation of 'reality' can be quite arbitrary; it is just a matter of rules. The soap-film analogy is a means to an end. It is a simple model that

produces a surface that has uniform tension in all directions. However, membrane structures are not built from soap films so these rules are arbitrary in their own right, dictated by the properties of the physical modelling medium. The uniform soap-film model may give us a 'pure' structural form but seldom satisfies the architectural requirements or artistic intent of a desired form.

By departing from physical analogies within the virtual world we experience more freedom to manipulate and engineer forms to our requirements while staying within the envelope of what is physically possible using materials and construction techniques at our disposal. The design of *Marsyas* by artist Anish Kapoor for the Tate Modern in 2002

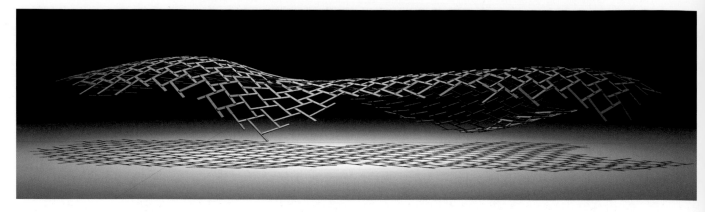

Shigeru Ban and Arup AGU, Forest Park Pavilion, St Louis, Missouri, 2005
Rendering of reciprocal timber roof.

involved developing a number of techniques during the concept period for defining, manipulating and engineering long-span highly nonuniform curved biomorphic forms.

The 'nonlinear soap film' was developed during the design of *Marsyas* as a method of controlling the tension in the warp and weft directions of the form independently and locally so producing areas to 'tailor' the form to the desired shape while retaining its structural integrity. The result is about as far from a uniform soap film as possible. Additional experiments during the design of *Marsyas* involved the combination of hydrostatic pressure and nonlinear surface tension, giving areas of synclastic and anticlastic curvature that yielded spectacular, if slightly unnerving biomorphic forms.

In a move aimed at gaining greater control over structurally realisable sculptural and architectural forms, the AGU has been looking at the other end of the spectrum, at some of the processes that have existed for hundreds of years in the patterning and tailoring of clothing. The process of starting with patterns that are laid on a mannequin or body and then adjusted/tailored to fit is almost the opposite of that used to produce membrane structures. However, by scrutinising this approach we have developed a method of taking a target form and using a new 'nip and tuck' algorithm within our form-finding software to modify local tensions and iteratively 'tailor' a form that closely matches the original target yet satisfies the requirement of having a minimum and maximum tension within the surface in order to maintain structural stability.

This year's Serpentine Pavilion at the Serpentine Gallery in Hyde Park is by architect Rem Koolhaas with Cecil Balmond and was designed using nip and tuck to create a 20-metre (66-foot) diameter, polycarbonate-clad hub capped with a floating, free-form 30-metre (98-foot) diameter helium-filled 'Cosmic Egg'.

The initial form had a very prominent dimple that would obviously wrinkle or even invert when inflated. The resulting nip-and-tucked form produced a stable, less extreme shape that still, however, retained a slightly anticlastic zone, highly unusual in inflated, lighter than air structures. The addition of almost 6,000 cubic metres (211,888 cubic feet) of helium also has a large impact on the overall form, pulling it skywards.

One of the main features of the Cosmic Egg is a rectangular volume subtracted from the underside of the inflated form and capped with a clear 10-square-metre (33-square-foot) ETFE 'window'. Because of the large distance and level of internal pressure the ETFE is not capable of spanning alone, and an orthogonal grid of polyester webbing belts was used to reinforce it, in effect producing a macrowoven coated material. The approach of adopting a primary and secondary structural system, standard practice in concrete and steel construction, allows tensile materials/fabrics to be mixed and matched for strength, transparency and other architectural and environmental requirements, thus broadening the scope of fabric structures and so constituting a key area of interest for the AGU.

Surface Mappings
Because the yarns within conventional structural fabrics are so small the material can be treated as a continuum. This allows 3-D surface models to be split and flattened into planar cutting patterns that can then be cut from the fabric and the seams stitched or welded together.

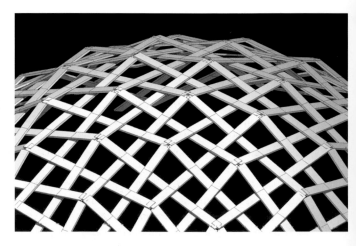

Arup AGU, Geometry research, 2006
Woven timber grid-shell geometry generated from four entwined orthogonal grids.

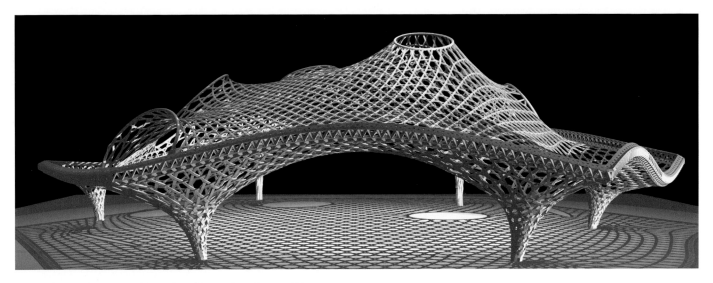

Shigeru Ban and Arup AGU, Pompidou Centre, Metz, France, 2005
Rendering of the woven, form-found roof.

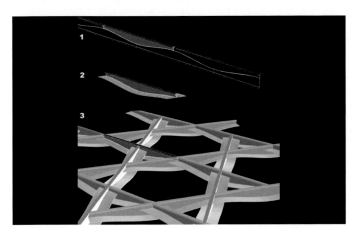

Three-way reciprocal beam arrangement: 1) Curved profiles cut from a single joist section; 2) Lower flange attached; 3) Insertion into the three-way grid using pin-ended connections.

However, if we want to move away from a material that can be treated as a continuum, eg if the scale of the cloth is increased to a net, then it becomes important that the individual 'yarns' between adjacent panels align, and so a different approach is needed.

The general problem of how to lay a continuous grid, structural system or arbitrary pattern over a surface is addressed in a process termed 'surface mapping' and is analogous to texture mapping in computer graphics. However, while texture mapping coordinates use a parameterisation of a mesh surface, independent of the mesh geometry, 'surface mapping' requires the use of uniform parameterisation (using real units) that is entirely dependent on mesh geometry.

A surface mapping technique is used by the AGU to design cable-net structures, grid shells and some 'macroweave' type shells as described below. The process involves form-finding a tensile soap film or hanging (compression) catenary surface to generate the appropriate structural form and then using bespoke software called ELM to map an equal-link-length mesh over the surface.

A simpler surface mapping technique was developed during the concept design of the Pompidou Metz roof to investigate basket-weaving techniques on a large scale.

The technique simulates the wrapping of straight flat ribbons (geodesics) over an arbitrary surface and is a method that can also be used for investigating trajectories for seam lines on fabric structures.

A new method of surface mapping currently undergoing development at the AGU attempts to create seamless arrangements for chain-mail type materials/structural systems over arbitrary surfaces. The process uses the principle of dynamic-relaxation (as used in its form-finding software) to distribute mutually attracting/repelling particles/nodes over a mesh surface. Using geodesic distances over the surface the nodes repel one another based on proximity, thus forming a highly efficient close-packed arrangement.

Macroweaving

In a move away from purely tensile form-finding and by investigating surface texture with structural pattern, in a number of recent projects the AGU has explored the application of the topology of weave to large-scale structural systems. This macroweaving is of discrete bending or compression shell elements rather than the microweaving of fabrics to form tension-only surfaces.

The projects have applied weaving to curved surfaces using bamboo and timber planks. They deviate from conventional timber grids-shells in that they employ different structural patterns, including reciprocal beams, and by allowing compression, tension and a degree of bending that can mix synclastic and anticlastic curvature. Work includes projects

Arup AGU, Weave Bridge, University of Pennsylvania, Philadelphia, 2006
Conceptual experiments in weaving elements of the Weave Bridge.

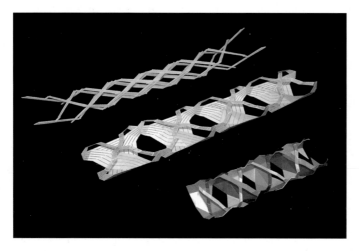

Models showing the design evolution of the structural elements of the Weave Bridge.

temporary works analogous to the loom. Then the structure would be jacked into position before connecting the layers together and thus locking the weave into the required geometry. This process is a development of the timber grid-shell technique best demonstrated in the Mannheim Multihalle. It was tested as an option for the construction of the Pompidou Metz roof, developed at competition stage by Shigeru Ban with AGU.

The second, and currently more fruitful approach is to reinterpret the literal weave and instead build the weave topology out of discrete elements – typically the length of two units of the weave grid. The result is a reciprocal grid that allows large spans to be created from short elements because they are arranged in this mutually supporting pattern. Rather than spanning by continuous grillage action, or through a hierarchical system of primary and secondary beams, the reciprocal grid provides a network of individual elements that act equally in the system. As the elements are mutually supporting, the load paths are of complex nested loops, superimposed throughout the network.

A traditional example of this is the timber lamella roof, developed by Zollinger in the 1920s, in which barrel vaults are built from short interlocking elements. The practical benefits of the system are in the handling of smaller components and the simplification of connections because no bending load need be transferred between elements.

AGU's first study of macroweaving was for the Forest Park Pavilion, St Louis, with architect Shigeru Ban. A proposal was made to build a roof using planks of laminated bamboo. As the plank length is limited to about 2 metres (6.5 feet) by the production technique, a reciprocal arrangement was developed. The system consists of pinwheels of overlapping planks that combine in a continuous pattern to generate a free-form roof. By choosing the orientation (under or over) of each overlap in each pinwheel the geometry can be controlled, allowing continuous variation between concave synclastic, anticlastic and convex synclastic double curvatures.

A more direct reading of weave was desired for the Pompidou Metz roof, where Ban was inspired by a traditional Chinese woven bamboo hat. The competition-stage proposal for the roof is a fabric-clad, single-layer grid shell in which the structural elements are based on a hexagonal pattern and use the reciprocal grid arrangement to simplify the connections. Each roof member is approximately 2.6 metres (8.5 foot) long with pin connections at each end joining to a point at the centre of its neighbouring elements. The depth of each steel element is greatest at its centre, where bending is greatest, and each element tapers towards its ends. This taper leads to a waving lower flange, which is formed in timber. In this way, the lower flanges of the beams appear to weave continuously throughout the roof.

The 2005 Serpentine Pavilion also used the reciprocal grid arrangement, in a form more directly related to the traditional lamella roof. The 400-square-metre (4,305-square-foot) building was formed from a grillage of laminated timber,

with Shigeru Ban and the 2005 Serpentine Pavilion by Alvaro Siza and Eduardo Souto de Moura with Cecil Balmond.

The aim of this work has been to exploit the structural benefits afforded by woven components – through weaving's network of mutual stiffening – and to produce new forms of geometric freedom of the surface through the articulation of the woven elements.

In attempting macroweave an immediate physical contradiction is encountered. While the mechanical process of weaving demands flexible elements to allow the warp and weft to become enmeshed, this inherent flexibility is seemingly at odds with the stiffness demanded by these structures for them to be able to resist bending or buckling under compression.

Two types of solution have been explored. The first requires that the literal interpretation of weave as the enmeshing of continuous elements is maintained, and that a stiff structure is built up by layering. For example, many very long strips of flexible laminated veneer lumber (LVL) could literally be woven together using an elaborate system of distorted in plan and profile in response to the surrounding landscape and neighbouring gallery building. The short elements interlocked in a mutually supporting pattern that was expressed through a shuffling offset in the grid. Simple mortice and tenon connections were used, despite the complex free-form geometry. Each of the 427 elements had a different length and inclination. The AGU defined their geometries by using a project-specific script and produced by a CNC robot at Finnforest Merk. The interlocking structure demanded that a unique erection sequence be defined, which was manifested in the detail of the connections.

Algorithms and Concepts

The processes described above indicate a move towards a loose interpretation between material, pattern and surface geometry. Rather than the reductionist dictum, favoured by many engineers, of 'form follows function', which hints at a single optimised solution to a design, the AGU approach is that material, pattern and geometry are threads that interweave in a complex semidependent way, converging on multiple viable solutions.

The key to being able to work on an abstract level with mathematics while iteratively evolving, searching and evaluating practical design solutions lies in the ability to program computers. From blending and projecting multidimensional objects through automating structural optimisation to the generation of CNC cutting patterns, some form of code is written on almost all AGU projects.

A current example of a project that exemplifies this way of working is the Weave Bridge commissioned for the University of Pennsylvania.

The concept for the bridge is a weave pattern of six different 'strips', winding from and unwinding back into the landscape to span 46 metres (150 feet) across the railway at the University of Pennsylvania. Two of the strips composing

this woven form unfold to become the cycle and the pedestrian paths, two strips geometrically continue into the balustrade handrails and two strips form the structural supports of the bridge at the abutments.

From concept stage the entire geometry was generated using procedural parameterised scripts in Rhino and then subsequently linked to structural analysis software to carry out structural design and optimisation of multiple design options.

In addition to the literal physical applications of weaving the mathematical description can be used in more abstract ways. The physical processes of weaving and knotting have abstract mathematical and procedural parallels. The underlying similarities lie within the use of a combined set of repetitive geometrical operations at differing levels of scale. One of the richest areas of investigation at the AGU is knots for use as architectural topological models in the organisation of space. Knot diagrams are simple and intuitive to use but are capable of giving rise to highly complex forms of space and structure.

The AGU has used geometric knots and Seifert surfaces to create single surface structures, such as that of the Arnhem Central project. Here a single knotted curve is used to define a complex nonorientable surface, where the traditional notions of floor, ceiling and wall are displaced by a form where no Cartesian reference system applies.

Future Fabric

Because new and exotic materials and fabrics are being created almost every day, what can be done with them is not limited by choice but rather by the available design techniques.

There is a large area of potential in the combination of multiple materials to form bespoke architectural 'fabric' that delivers structural strength, stiffness, weatherproofing, insulation, power, heat and light to exactly where it is required.

Inspiration at the high-tech end of the scale currently exists in the design and fabrication of bespoke 3-D curved sails for performance racing yachts which are made by laminating individually placed aramid yarns between layers of film on a CNC former. Inspiration at the more robust construction end of the scale comes from techniques being researched and developed for the rapid manufacturing of mass-market prefab buildings. Here the promise is for the entire building to be built layer by layer by robot, in theory depositing different materials and components as it proceeds.

Unlike the lucrative sponsorship of international yachting and the big-business finance behind mass-market housing, AGU's R&D is motivated by the drive to explore new territories within architecture and engineering, and the wish to rise to individual design challenges on a project by project basis. AGU has to thank Arup, its collaborators and clients, for their foresight, ambition and support. ⚙

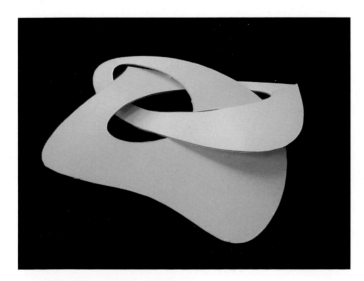

Arup AGU, Geometry research, 2002
Trefoil knot model.

Cutty Sark, Greenwich, London

Grimshaw + Youmeheshe

Cutty Sark is the world's most famous clipper ship and, since being opened to the public in 1957, has been a key attraction of the Maritime Greenwich World Heritage Site. The project has received approval for a Heritage Lottery Fund grant to reinvigorate the visitor experience and facilitate the conservation of the deteriorating vessel.

This innovative design, developed by architects Youmeheshe in association with Grimshaw, proposes to lift Cutty Sark within her dry berth. This will provide a large area for visitors to pass under her elegant hull, the most significant yet least appreciated part of the ship. Temporary enclosures and structures will allow visitors to witness the conservation work that will take place over the next few years.

The original design was for an ETFE temporary enclosure, as illustrated here, with a series of entwined air-filled columns supporting the canopy. These tubes are also of ETFE with a thin steel strip running along opposing sides. The resulting composite member has remarkable rigidity and remains incredibly lightweight. The system, developed by Airlite, has even been used to support road bridges in France. Single-layer ETFE is extended between the metal strips of the air-filled columns to form the facade.

Christopher Nash, Grimshaw

Nirah, Bedford, UK

Grimshaw

Nirah's mission is to promote understanding of the connection between fresh water and life. It will raise public awareness of the manmade destruction of freshwater environments through dams, extraction and pollution. The project will consist of huge aquaria together with research and education facilities on a 101-hectare (250-acre) brownfield site of disused clay pits near Bedford. The holistic premise drives the design response, where water, earthworks and landscape combine beneath a series of cloud-like transparent ETFE roofs. The appearance of the roofs corresponds with their function; as the size of the enclosure increases, they become proportionately more undulating to provide structural integrity. The ripples of the lower pathway canopies give way to increasingly curvaceous roofs that culminate in the large tropical Biotope, which provides a stunning silhouette on the Bedfordshire skyline.

Grimshaw has worked closely with Nirah's project director, Ronnie Murning, and Arup, SKM Anthony Hunts, Grant Associates and Davis Langdon on the design concept. ⏁

Jolyon Brewis, Grimshaw

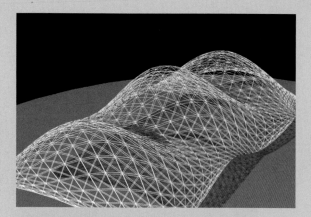

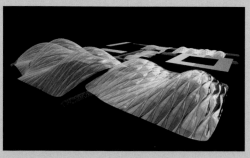

Tambabox, Tambacounda, Senegal

ex.studio

To the east of Dakar, where the landscape extends in the savannah, is Tambacounda, capital of Eastern Senegal, which groups together three departments: Tambacounda, Bakel and Kédougou. Economically the region is one of the country's poorest, but culturally one of its richest. Tambacounda's great cultural wealth is due to its geographic situation. On the one hand its traditions and customs are preserved, yet at the same time it is a place of multicultural dynamic encounter, the result of sharing its borders with five other countries: Gambia, Mali, Mauritania, Guinea Konakry and Guinea Bissau.

Tambabox is an object-space created from the extraordinarily varied and complex world of industrial textiles that most of the Senegalese use to make their own *boubous* (traditional clothing). The project consists of the creation of an inner space enveloped by an assembly of textile canvases. The textiles that delimit this architecture are murals in which the body is partly transformed, becoming part of the linen cloth: complex fragments that describe the variety of the landscape and its people, towns that coexist in its markets, its cities, or its vast and wide horizon.

Tambabox emerges from the landscape looking for an almost impossible intimate place; it defines a new place, contrasting with the concept of construction and the landscape of the surroundings related to the open spaces of ample horizons.

The piece works like a structure interposed between the sunlight and the interior space it encloses. The textile planes are regulators of light, filters that sift natural light from the outside. During the day, lighting in the space varies through different reflections and colourations, with light figures developing through the fading backgrounds. At night the space is transformed into an illuminated polychromatic box, contrasting with the intense darkness. From the textile canvas, projected shadows of bodies are revealed from the interior.

The space is a static piece which, in contact with the body, becomes an animated object as a provocation transmitted by the skin. The result is a space where sculpture, architecture and movement come together – a project that explores the space through the corporeal experience of the people – and has the capability to fragment into multiple pieces that disperse through the walls of the city.

The project was realised in 2005 as a collaboration between ex.studio architects Iván Juárez and Patricia Meneses and local craftsmen, carpenters and tailors – fundamental characters of great tradition in Senegal. It was proposed as an open space where practitioners of different art disciplines – dancers, musicians, actors and painters – could take part in the same poetry. Δ

Iván Juárez and Patricia Meneses

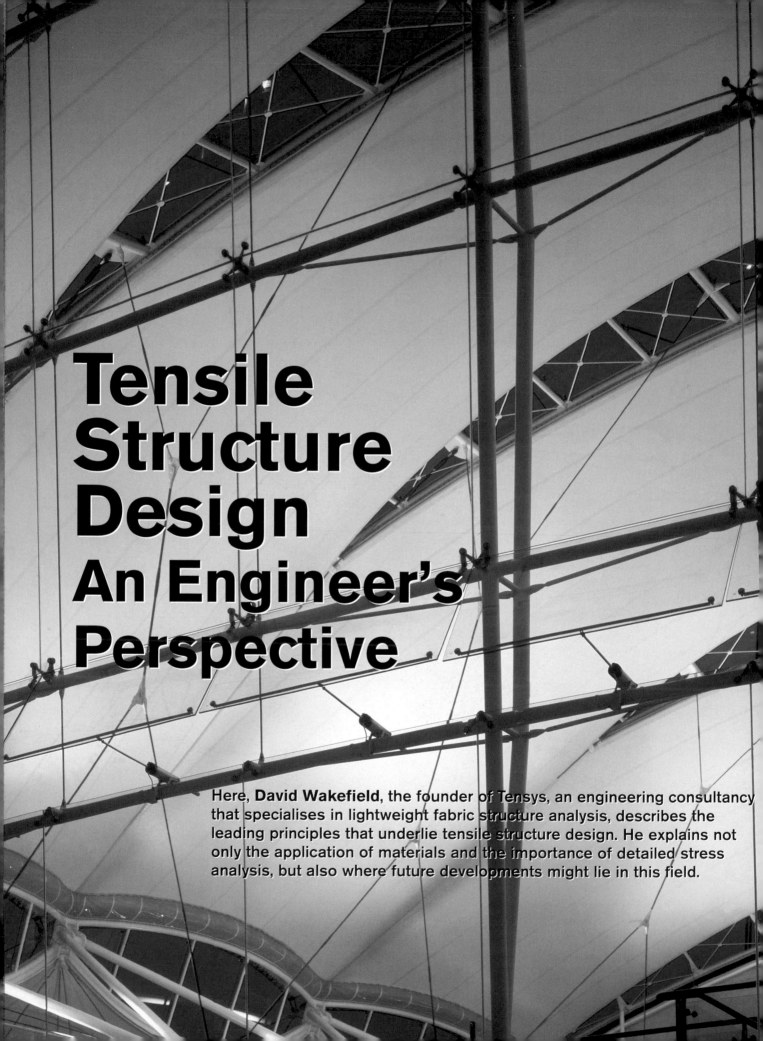

Tensile Structure Design
An Engineer's Perspective

Here, **David Wakefield**, the founder of Tensys, an engineering consultancy that specialises in lightweight fabric structure analysis, describes the leading principles that underlie tensile structure design. He explains not only the application of materials and the importance of detailed stress analysis, but also where future developments might lie in this field.

The use of fabric in building, both for simple shade and complete structures, has a long history. Basic shade, to designs that have not changed over many centuries, may still be seen in the side streets of southern Europe and Arabia. Tents as complete enclosures have an equally long history, and are still utilised as dwellings by nomadic peoples such as the Bedouin and Mongols. Modern tents more typically provide temporary accommodation, whether recreational or for refugee camps or places of pilgrimage. Ideas of demountability and retraction are associated with the flexibility and light weight of the basic material. Beyond individual dwellings, larger tents were built as pavilions for exhibitions and bazaars in styles that have evolved towards the traditional circus 'big top'.

The modern impetus for building with textiles was stimulated by the work of the German architect Frei Otto. From his early shade sails, to the roofs for the Munich Olympics and the Diplomatic Club in Riyadh, Otto has explored lightness and efficiency in construction through the study of the evolution of forms in nature. The classic minimal surface he championed is that of the membrane stressed uniformly in all directions, as exemplified by his soap-film models.

Architectural interest in the use of materials grew in parallel with developments in materials technology. Increasing strength and improved coatings enabled structural fabrics to carry significant loads without compromising appearance. Sports venues and leisure facilities have led the way, driven by the need to cover large spaces while maintaining a good quality of light and visual flair, examples of which include the large air-supported roofs built in the US in the 1980s and, more recently, the majority of stadia built for the football world cups in Asia and Europe. The lightness of the enclosing membrane has encouraged a similar lightness in the supporting primary structure.

However, not all applications are canopy roofs. Structural fabrics are now integrated into the building enclosure, for example in the Inland Revenue Amenity Building in Nottingham and the Burj al Arab Hotel in Dubai.

Membranes for Tensile Structures

Three principal materials are currently in use: PVC-coated polyester and PTFE-coated glass are coated woven fabrics capable of carrying significant structural loads, and ETFE film is a thin, clear, extruded film applied primarily for cladding applications in the form of multilayer inflated cushions.

PVC-coated polyester is used for a wide range of projects where a life span of greater than 20 years is not required. Various surface coatings are available to improve its environmental resistance, and its relative flexibility when

Their flexibility of construction has made tents the most common demountable buildings over many centuries. These recreational pavilions provide shelter for an 1848 official dinner in Clapham. Their similarity to marquees of today may readily be seen.

Michael Hopkins and Partners and Arup, Inland Revenue Amenity Building, Nottingham, 1994
The building features membrane and glazing integrated into its fabric to provide a light and welcoming environment.

Atkins and Tensys, Burj al Arab Hotel, Dubai, 1999
The hotel features a facade wall with two layers of PTFE-coated glass-fibre structural membrane that controls the light entering the full-height atrium.

Grimshaw and Partners, Arup and Tensys, National Space Centre rocket tower, Leicester, 2001
The tower is an example of the imaginative use of ETFE foil cushions as building cladding. Opened in 2001, it was designed by Nicholas Grimshaw and Partners with engineering by Arup and final analysis and patterning by Tensys on behalf of membrane contractor Skyspan Europe.

Murphy/Jahn, Suvarnabhumi Airport, Bangkok, Thailand, 2006
The concourses at Bangkok's new international airport feature alternating modules of glazing and multilayer membrane construction. The latter has a PTFE-coated glass outer membrane, a cable-net/polycarbonate sheet mid-layer for acoustic damping, and a low-emissivity inner liner.

folded makes it suitable for retractable membranes. PTFE-coated woven glass fibre has a significantly longer life expectancy and a self-cleansing surface. Although greater care has to be taken with detailing and handling of the membrane, this has become the material of choice for major permanent structures. Because of its glass base cloth, it is not suited to retractable roofs involving membrane folding. However, the replacement of the glass base weave with PTFE fibres has produced a specialist all-PTFE material that is particularly suited to repeated folding and also offers a very good quality of light – albeit at a price premium compared to the standard products. Lastly, ETFE foil is gaining popularity as a geometrically flexible lightweight cladding alternative to glass, its application brought to the fore through the success of the Eden Project in Cornwall.

Material developments are focused on improving the performance of existing products with the application of new coating technologies to improve cleansing, and acoustic and energy transmission properties. For example, the recently completed new Bangkok international airport features concourse roofs with a multilayer approach to provide an overall performance requirement. An outer layer of PTFE-coated glass membrane and an inner layer of fluropolymer-coated glass with perforations for sound absorption and a low-emissivity coating encapsulate a cable net supporting polycarbonate sheets for further acoustic control.

The Design Process

Tensile membrane structures carry loads by direct forces within their components in either tension (fabric and cables) or compression (masts and struts). By avoiding bending, the materials are used to their maximum efficiency. With all loads carried within the surface of a membrane, the distribution and magnitude of stresses are dependent on the shape of the membrane. Put simply, the engineering of a membrane structure is its shape. The magnitude of stress within a membrane or cable subject to loading perpendicular to its surface is proportional to the curvature of the surface – the flatter the surface, the higher the stress. The amount of deflection induced is dependent upon both the curvature and the amount of prestress, or permanent stress, in the membrane.

Surfaces exhibiting 'negative' curvature, whereby the principal curvature in one direction acts in an opposite sense to that in the other, are the most commonly used. Cones, saddle shapes and hyperbolic paraboloids maintain prestress by the force balance between these two directions. Up and down loads are carried in one direction or the other. Membranes with 'positive' curvature, such as domes, require the addition of inflation pressure to maintain both the shape and prestress. Up loads are carried by the membrane acting in tension; down loads require sufficient inflation pressure to resist them while maintaining stability.

A close interaction between engineer and architect is essential from the earliest stages of design. The form, or shape, of the structure needs to satisfy aesthetic, functional and engineering requirements. A typical design cycle starts with determination of a basic form, subjecting that form to structural and functional analysis and evaluating the results. If unacceptable, the form is modified and the iterative cycle repeated. Otherwise, the process moves on to the final detailing and production of fabrication information.

All elements of a membrane structure are exposed to view, and careful consideration must therefore be given to the function and appearance of the detail components that provide the attachment between membrane, cables and the supporting primary structure. The engineering design of membrane structures should be regarded as 'different', rather than 'difficult', when compared with other structural types. The materials are relatively unfamiliar and their lack of bending stiffness means that the structures undergo significant deformations in order to carry load, which requires care in the detailing and geometrically nonlinear analysis techniques.

Structure Modelling

Since the early work of Frei Otto, models have played a significant part in the design of tension structures. The flexibility of simple models using stretch fabric provides a rapid tool for exploring the validity and appearance of a three-dimensional membrane surface. The design of the Olympic roofs in Munich was heavily dependent on photogrammetric investigations of scale models. Although physical models are still used, particularly for initial architectural studies and client presentations, computer modelling is now the principal tool for analysis and construction.

The basic requirements of any design software for membrane structures are rooted in the need to first determine an appropriate equilibrium form, to analyse the response of that form under applied loading and to produce membrane cutting patterns and cable schedules that enable the accurate replication of the form in construction.

Analysis software is based on the finite-element method, a numerical technique whereby the membrane surface is subdivided into a large number of triangular elements, its geometry defined by the spatial coordinates of the triangle corners that are also the node points at which adjacent triangles are connected. Cables are subdivided into a series of line elements between intermediate nodes that coincide with those of the connecting membrane. The mathematical approximation lies in the assumption of constant stress within individual elements, and thus the accuracy of the numerical model may be increased by increasing the number of finite elements representing a particular structure.

With knowledge of the material properties, the stresses in individual elements are calculated according to the deformation caused by relative deflections of their connecting nodes. Deflection of those nodes is a function of the total forces exerted on them by all the connected elements. Such calculations must be undertaken simultaneously for all elements (which can number tens of thousands) in order to find a combination of element stresses and node positions that represent a stable equilibrium state.

The inTENS software developed by Tensys uses a method called Dynamic Relaxation to solve these equations. The details of this method are not as important as its ability to be readily understood and not place restrictions on design possibilities because of limited analytical capability. The latter is particularly relevant at the shape-finding stage, when shapes may be adjusted by varying the magnitude and ratios of principal stresses within the membrane surface.

inTENS allows membrane stress ratios to be varied throughout the surface, with directional control provided by the simultaneous generation of geodesic trajectories in the chosen directions of principal curvature. This flexibility was essential in deriving the equilibrium surfaces of complex structural forms exemplified by the recent *Marsyas* sculpture and Spiky Pod projects. inTENS has been specifically developed to encourage the freedom to investigate a wide range of possible surface forms and to test their structural viability.

New Developments

Future developments rest primarily in the areas of materials development and applications. The basic analytical tools necessary to cover shape generation are already available. And improvements are under way for more sophisticated representations of material properties that will enable the influence of installation methodology on stress distribution and structure response to be considered, and greater design certainty when integrated into reliability analyses. Techniques developed within the architectural membrane structures field are also forming the basis for geometric and materially nonlinear analyses of high-altitude scientific balloons and hybrid air vehicles.

However, in architecture, the main recent development is the growing popularity of ETFE-film cushions for cladding as at the Eden Project, Allianz Arena in Munich and the Aquatic Centre for the Beijing Olympics. The combination of efficient yet aesthetically satisfying, lightweight construction methods with energy-saving technologies has significant possibilities for facades and shading. Current-generation photovoltaic cells might be encapsulated within ETFE cushions, with newer devices expected to become coatings for flexible membranes.

The use of structural membranes has steadily evolved since they first became popular in the late 1970s and early 1980s. With the associated development of materials, practical experience and design capabilities the firm foundations of what is now effectively a 'standard' construction option have been established. New designers, applications and ideas must now be encouraged to exploit this knowledge and reinvigorate its application to the challenges of function, appearance and efficiency. ∆

Y-Knots, Mile End and the Lower Lee Valley, East London

Mark Garcia + Jonathan Goslan

Garcia and Goslan's investigations into the spatial possibilities of knot theory have led to their collaboration on a number of projects using the freeware programme Knotplot. For Gotfried Semper, the knot was the first architectural joint. The idea of turning a joint (as a single detail) into an entire structure is the objective of this study. After digitally generating the topography of the knots, two projects for London's East End – the Mile End Centre (on the banks of the Grand Union Canal) and the Olympic Information Centre (in the Lower Lee Valley) – were developed as diagrammatic sketches. The forms hover over the ground, suspended from their minimal footprints. The structural anchorings double up as separated, independent entry points distributed across the open public spaces beneath the forms. As the large, muscular, torqued cantilevers swerve out over the landscape, they increase the space available on the upper levels, allowing for circulation throughout the structure and providing panoramic views out over London. Supported by a mesh of steel and carbon-fibre beams, this fabric supports the flat quadrilateral panels of the pixel-like exterior envelopes (Teflon and glass) and internal plates. Addressing the past and present sociocultural contexts of their sites, the knotted forms refer to the historic textile and rope factories in the area, Islamic geometry, braided Afro hairstyles, the knotting of muscles and the joining of nations (the de/reconstructed Olympic rings) for the London Olympics 2012. △

Mark Garcia and Jonathan Goslan

An Embellishment: Purdah

Jane Rendell

I spent my childhood in the Middle East, in Afghanistan, Ethiopia, Sudan and the United Arab Emirates. Remembering those times brings to mind spatial images of thresholds and boundaries. I am there, in those scenes, engaged in tracing the edges of surfaces – carpets, dresses, walls, floors.

In the Middle East, the term 'purdah' describes the cultural practice of separating and hiding women, through clothing and architecture – veils, screens and walls – from the public gaze. The particular manifestation of this gendering of space varies depending on location. For example, in Afghanistan, under the Taliban, in public women were required to wear a burqa, in this case a loose garment, usually sky blue, that covered them from head to foot. Only their eyes could be seen (the rims outlined, but perhaps only in a Westerner's imagination, with black kohl) looking out through the window of an embroidered screen.

For An Embellishment: Purdah, as part of the 'Spatial Imagination' exhibition at the Domo Baal Gallery in London in January 2006,[1] I repeatedly wrote the word 'purdah' in black kohl on a west-facing window in the script of Afghanistan's official languages – Dari and Pashto. By day or by night, from inside the gallery or from outside on the street, the work changed according to the viewer's position – transparent/opaque, concealing/revealing – the embellishment, or decorative covering, invited the viewer to imagine beyond the places he or she could see. 𝒟

Note
1. Jane Rendell, An Embellishment: Purdah, 'Spatial Imagination' (London: The Domo Baal Gallery, 2006) with an associated catalogue essay in Peg Rawes and Jane Rendell (eds), *Spatial Imagination*, the Bartlett School of Architecture, UCL (London), 2005.

Jane Rendell

Textiles for 21st-Century Living

Here, **Marie O'Mahony** focuses on one of the most exciting areas of innovation for textiles – the hybridisation of materials and engineering techniques. It is, as she explains, the very blurring of what a textile constitutes that opens up so many possibilities for material science and application in architecture.

The world of materials has never been more exciting, subject to a constant flow of new developments and transformations. The notion of what constitutes a fibre or fabric has been thrown open for debate. If it looks like a textile, feels like a textile and behaves like one, does this make it a textile? Under this criterion, a whole host of nontextile and hybrid materials from ceramic to glass can, on occasion, be regarded as textiles. This makes it a very exciting time for designers who can now find solutions not only in the textile mill, but also in the biotechnologist's laboratory or zoological garden. We are already seeing the impact of this on textile design, as well as on the use of textiles in a range of disciplines from fashion to product design and architecture.

Engineered Fibres and Fabrics

The engineering of fibres and fabrics has accelerated over the past decade. What is now possible is driven by the imagination. Whatever one can think of, a fibre or fabric engineer somewhere around the world is probably already working on it. Traditional blended fibres have given way to developments such as Toyobo's Air Cube hollow nylon fibre that uses air to provide thermal insulation. Flat fabrics that go on to form three-dimensional stitched garments or objects have given way to fabrics that can be sprayed on to the body to create garments and semiliving clothes that are grown on to a fabric substrate. And even traditional processes are not exempt from the impact of technology. Weaving looms and knitting machines now allow three-dimensional fabrics to be produced, often using technical fibres (such as carbon and glass), which little more than a decade ago were extremely difficult and expensive to work with, causing frequent breakages of equipment. Even embroidery has been transformed and is no longer simply a mode of surface decoration. For example, Ellis Developments has adapted the technology for industrial and medical applications. Stitched on to a soluble fabric substrate. The embroidery is treated to become rigid, and the fabric substrate dissolved resulting in a very lightweight but strong structure.

Hybrid Materials

The emergence of hybrid materials has seen the textile industry move far beyond the mixing of natural and synthetic fibres, instead bringing together textiles and nontextiles. This can typically be a combination of fibre with ceramic, glass or even metal. The benefit of this approach is the development of highly efficient materials that use the specific qualities of both textile and nontextile. Glass fibre is one of the most common. This is extruded molten glass drawn to form strands that can then be treated as fibres. Woven, or in nonwoven mats, they are further treated to add performance and make them safer to handle. Prized for its excellent heat resistance and strength, it is used for

Oron Catts and Ionat Zurr, Prototype of stitchless jacket grown in a technoscientific body, Tissue Culture and Art project, University of Western Australia, 2003
The semiliving jacket uses biotechnology to combine human and mouse connective tissue. The jacket is grown inside a bell jar on a biodegradable fabric substrate that provides the scaffolding for the jacket to grow. Once exposed to bacteria, the garment is destroyed.

industrial applications and architectural membranes. In its nonwoven form it can be used as the basis for lightweight but strong composites in everything from chairs to automotive applications.

Metal fibres and fabrics can often take on a silk-like appearance in terms of drape and lustre. They can also be used to help create a low-relief, three-dimensional fabric. Pure metal fibres are heavy, but synthetics that have been coated with a fine layer of metal have a similar weight to traditional synthetics. Metallised fibres can be woven, knitted, and produced as nonwovens and tape. Applications vary from protective lining for walls (where the metal fibre is applied much like wallpaper) to shirts and even underwear to protect the occupant or wearer from harmful electromagnetic rays.

Carbon fibre initially came to prominence in the manufacture of products that required a material that combined lightness, strength and high fatigue-resistance. Used as part of a composite structure, applications range from aerospace to sports equipment. It has recently attracted interest because of its conductive properties. Conductive fibres are being incorporated into woven fabrics to be used in wearable technology products.

Donut seat using spacer fabric by Sachio Hinara with Margareta Zetterblom's Quiet sound-absorbing fabric panels behind. Both exhibited at the Advanced Fabrics Exhibition, IFAI, Texas, 2005.

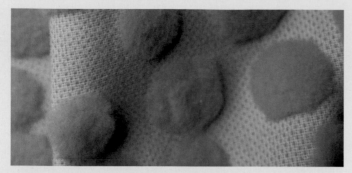

Pharenta 3-D tufted fabric used as a paint-roller fabric to provide pattern when rolling paint on a wall or ceiling.

Andrea Valentini's polyurethane Acoustic Panels are part of her ongoing research into the problem of providing acoustic insulation in an aesthetic way.

Palmhive's Bobble Camouflage is a 3-D warp knitted fabric used by the military as a stealth fabric. When placed over tanks it allows them to avoid radar detection.

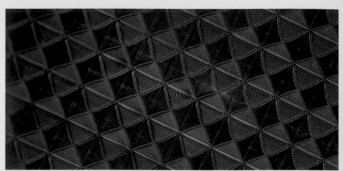

Verasol's 3-D metallic fabric is used in window blinds to provide solar shade. The polyester fabric is aluminised and formed in a low-relief diamond pattern.

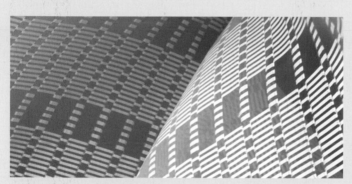

Nuno Corporation, Windbreak, 2005. Cut weaving involves 'floating' loose thread structures that are then cut either by hand or machine. Here, the transparency of monofilament threads and fringes are first rough-cut by hand, then evened off with a cropping machine.

Green-Tek's Aluminet is a hortisynthetic fabric used to protect young plants from overheating in strong sunlight. The synthetic yarns have an aluminised coating.

Verasol's metallic print is embossed on a synthetic coated with metal and designed for use in window blinds to provide solar shade.

Stomatex Ltd has developed a unique neoprene with tiny convex bumps that pushes moisture away from the body.

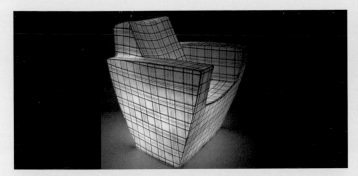

Critz Campbell uses a glass-fibre composite and antique fabrics in his Eudora chair, which is illuminated from within.

Hil Driessen, crochet ceramic bowl from the Into Focus collection produced at the European Ceramic Research Centre.

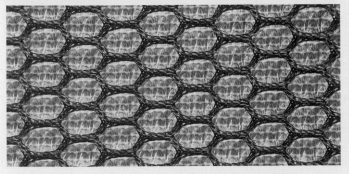

Hybrid + Fusion's 3-D knitted spacer fabrics combine performance with aesthetics.

Nuno Corporation, Vines, 2005. Twisting and turning creepers stitch the forest together. Rustic vines, much sought after for crafting flower baskets, are replicated in shiny taffeta tapes creating a beautiful semitransparent embroidery.

Lesley Sealey layers preprinted fabric with nonwovens and an overprint of glitter to transform the ordinary.

Nuno Corporation, Weathered Bark, 2005. A portrait of an ancient trunk in the Aokigahara Jukai Sea of Trees at the foot Mount Fuji in Yamanashi where this tapestry was actually crafted. Stainless-steel threads woven into the underside add a quiet sheen to the fabric.

Hil Driessen has developed a range of fabrics based on work at the European Ceramic Work Centre. Crochet bowls were dipped in porcelain, fired and computer scanned before printing and weaving the designs. Shown here is a Jacquard weave from the series woven at the Textielmuseum in Tilburg.

Smartslab uses an aluminium honeycomb as the basis for this composite. LEDs are inserted into the hexagonal honeycomb to provide an extremely sharp pixilated image inspired by the eye of the fly.

Tate in Space

ETALAB

ETALAB's proposal for a Tate in Space[1] responds to the extreme environment of outer space and the unpredictable needs of artists, curators and visitors. The gallery exists in microgravity with the possibility of introducing artificial gravity by varying the speed of rotation about a central axis. The envelope is made from smart materials, based on biomimetics, to create a continuously evolving form, allowing artists and curators the freedom to modify the form, space and levels of gravity across the gallery. Visitors can move freely in all directions, without the restrictions of staircases or lifts. Windows, seamlessly integrated into the skin, expand and contract like the lens of an eye to present the visual wonder of the universe and magnified views back to earth.

The intelligent skin is made from a multistranded cross weave of single-purpose hi-technology microfibres combined with pneumatic actuators and a state-of-the-art interface. Sensors embedded within the skin are capable of responding locally to stimuli such as the movement of people, sound, light and electronic signals, creating an ever-changing and dynamic environment. These biomimetic properties, operating like muscles and the nervous system, allow for responsive control over the colour, transparency and translucency of the envelope.

A 3-D computer model would enable artists and curators to test their ideas and then apply them to the physical Tate in Space. Similarly, online visitors would be able to access the interactive model and create their own version of Tate in Space including personal virtual exhibitions.

The gallery would dock at the International Space Station (ISS) or make solo voyages across the solar system, transforming into a solar sail for sustainable propulsion. Visitors should have easy and affordable access to the ISS by the time the new Tate is completed, making Tate in Space the ultimate destination gallery.

Developed in consultation with scientists, the gallery uses advanced technology materials such as: Nextel, a high-strength ceramic material with high insulation performance, capable of withstanding extremely high temperatures (up to +250°C/+482°F in space); carbon fibres and nanotube (carbon fibres are high strength with high temperature resistance, and carbon nanotube ceramic composites are in development); shape memory alloys which change their crystal structure according to temperature changes (these would function as actuators pulling the skin in certain directions and could be linked to commands relating to the speed of rotation and hence level of gravity); artificial collagen, which could provide the translucency, transparency and optical properties for the lens-like windows; and Kevlar, for impact resistance against space debris and meteorites and temperature resistance of -250°C/-482°F. Light-emitting diodes (LEDs) based on molecules that emit light (photons) when an electrical current is applied are set on the inside of the skin like jewels on a fabric to provide light and display functions, and the external skin incorporates a mosaic of thin-film silicon solar cells which allows the building's large external surface area to function as a solar collector and power the gallery. Δ

Note

1. Based in London and New York, ETALAB (Extra-Terrestrial Architecture Laboratory) was founded by Opher Elia-Shaul and Danielle Tinero in 2002, and was one of three architectural firms invited by artist Susan Collins to design visionary proposals for a 21st-century Tate gallery in space. Tate in Space, conceived by artist Susan Collins as a site-specific artwork for the Tate website and commissioned in 2002 as part of its Netart series, is located at www.tate.org.uk/space.

Opher Elia-Shaul and Danielle Tinero

02 virtual artworks and ETALAB

Bio-Tissue Hotel

Stefanie Surjo

Biotechnologies are changing the way designers create objects, the thinking processes of making, and the social, aesthetic, technical and cultural implications of art and architecture. Objects such as fabrics/textiles are no longer dependent on manufacturing processes, but can be grown in accordance with natural biological processes. The Bio-Tissue Hotel (Diploma second-year project, UCL, 2005) was developed to explore the concept of a 'living surface' as an architectural fabric/structure/materiality – a cultured-skin architectural technology.

The culture of skin, which is the growing of skin or a skin substitute outside of the human body, is one of the key achievements of biotechnology, which could be adapted to manufacture biological textiles. The idea of biological textiles is just one example of how semiliving surfaces could soon exist and find applications in other forms of designed objects. The existence of a semiliving biotextile skin could provide a new type of solution to our desire for a more complex relationship to our environment. The aesthetic and responsiveness of different types of animal skins offer a particularly interesting source of forms and interactive functionalities for possible architectural biotextile skins. This project for a future hotel examines the revolutionary possibilities of the application of these material qualities.

The Bio-Tissue Hotel, Shanghai, China, assumes a future scenario where designers would benefit from biotechnologically related textile products such as an artificial living architectural skin. The pockets contained in its organic facade are hotel rooms that provide an intermediate environment for interaction with semiliving surfaces made from a variety of artificially grown biological skins. This living surface could eventually cover a variety of objects and architectural surfaces, or could simply be an independent entity of its own.

The living textile skins provide visual, tactile, emotional, intimate and pleasing messages about the object that can stimulate new types of behavioural, emotional and perceptual experiences in users. Though apparently uncanny, long-term interaction with the semiliving skin could become merely a matter of familiarity. In the future this extraordinary invention would become no more common than the ordinary everyday object. The Bio-Tissue Hotel project proposes that biotextiles and semiliving surfaces will change the way designers define aesthetic form, and the ways of making and building, altering our understanding in both objects and the construction of the body at its most intimate level. ∆

Stefanie Surjo

Contributors

Will Alsop is an internationally renowned architect, artist, designer, writer and academic. A Stirling Prize winner, he has led an international practice (now SMC Alsop) for more than 30 years. He has held many international academic posts including his long-term post as a visiting professor of architecture at the RCA.

Ron Arad's constant experimentation with the use and possibilities of materials such as steel, aluminium and polyamide, and his radical reconception of the form and structure of furniture has put him at the forefront of contemporary design. His current architectural commissions range from large hotel projects to a design museum in Israel. He is the winner of numerous design awards and his work appears in many public collections.

Charlie de Bono is a London-based freelance architect and designer, and a graduate of Edinburgh University and the Bartlett, UCL. He is a founder of the Dirty Atelier, and a member of the EASA community, where he has tutored at the 'emancipated b*st*rds' workshop.

Daniel Bosia is an architect and structural engineer who works with Cecil Balmond at Arup, collaborating with architects such as Daniel Libeskind, Toyo Ito and Enric Miralles. He is a co-founder of the Advanced Geometry Unit at Arup, where he is leading several bridge designs and projects within the Battersea Masterplan in London.

Nigel Coates co-founded the NATO (Narrative Architecture Today) group in 1983. His practice Branson Coates Architecture has completed many projects in Japan, the UK and Europe, including the National Centre for Popular Music in Sheffield and the Body Zone in the Millennium Dome, London. He is also a professor of architectural design at the RCA.

Opher Elia-Shaul and **Danielle Tinero** are architects and co-founders of ETALAB. Elia-Shaul's work has covered residential, commercial, leisure and retail sectors and masterplanning. His specialisations include museum and cultural buildings, and intelligent building applications. Tinero has worked for world-class architects (Fosters, KPF and Alsop Architects) on major London office developments, transportation, sports, residential, arts and education projects. She designed the Lister Mills project with David Morley.

Kathryn Findlay worked for Arata Isozaki before establishing the Ushida Findlay Partnership in Japan with Eisaku Ushida in 1996, and Ushida Findlay in the UK in 1998. She has sinced established an innovative form of research-based practice, Fieldwork, partnered between Ushida Findlay and the University of Dundee.

Massimiliano Fuksas has practices in Rome, Paris, Vienna and Frankfurt. He won the Grand Prix d'Architecture Française in 1999, and was curator of the Venice Architecture Biennale in 2000. His recent works include the New Trade Fair Milan, Congress Hall in Rome-Eur and the Peres Centre for Peace in Jaffa, Israel.

Mark Garcia is the academic coordinator in the Department of Architecture at the RCA. He has lectured on the RCA-wide MPhil/PhD Research Methods Course and teaches spatial design theory and design research methodologies. His current projects focus on the relationships between architectural/urban design and fashion/textile design, and on contemporary spatial design theory and the visualisation of art and design research methodologies, the architectural diagram and sketch, and on play, games and toys in architecture.

Jonathan Goslan is a sculptor, digital artist and musician. He has exhibited with young artists in London and New York, and more recently has been developing an innovative and extensive range of geometrical sculptural forms generated from CAD and CAM. He is co-founder of the practice Abject Object.

Nicholas Grimshaw's practice was founded in London in 1980, and now has branch offices in New York and Melbourne. The practice's portfolio covers all major sectors and includes the Eden Project in Cornwall and the International Terminal at Waterloo station in London.

Iván Juárez and **Patricia Meneses** are the founders of Barcelona practice ex.studio. Their projects explore the relationship between art and function, integrating the disciplines of architecture, design, sculpture and installation. Their projects and exhibitions investigate and experiment with new ways of relating space with society.

Robert Kronenburg holds the Chair of Architecture at Liverpool School of Architecture, Liverpool University. His books include *Houses in Motion* (Wiley-Academy, 2002), and he is co-editor of the *Transportable Environments* series (Spon Press). He also curated the RIBA exhibition 'Portable Architecture'. His book *Flexible: Architecture that Responds to Change* will be published in 2007.

Matilda McQuaid is deputy curatorial director and head of the textiles department at the Smithsonian's Cooper-Hewitt, National Design Museum, and was formerly at MoMA. Her most recent show, 'Extreme Textiles: Designing for High Performance', was the first major museum exhibition devoted to high-performance fabrics and their applications in areas such as architecture, aerospace, medicine and sports.

Yusuke Obuchi, **Theodore Spyropoulos** and **Tom Verebes** co-direct the Design Research Lab (DRL) at the AA, a postprofessional masters programme focusing on the potential of material and digital modes of computation and their application towards the production of parametric forms of architecture and urbanism.

Marie O'Mahony is a textile and technology consultant and advises architects, designers and manufacturers on advanced materials. She also curates international exhibitions, events and workshops, and has written several books on the impact of technology on textiles.

David Morley founded his own practice in 1987 after 11 years at Fosters. David Morley Architects has won a multitude of prestigious awards, including the 'Young Architecture Practice of the Year' in 2002. He has lectured at many universities, and is an awards and competitions assessor for RIBA and NHS Estates.

Dominique Perrault has offices in Paris, Luxembourg and Madrid. His current commissions include the expansion of the European Court of Justice in Luxembourg and the Olympic tennis stadium in Madrid. He has been a professor at many schools of architecture, and awards include the Mies van der Rohe Pavilion Award for European Architecture.

Bradley Quinn is an author and curator based in New York. His books include *The Fashion of Architecture* (Berg Publishers, 2003), and current projects include a forthcoming book on material intelligence and a report on the role of apparel and textiles in disaster relief for the office of the UN High Commissioner for Refugees.

Sally Quinn studied at Edinburgh University and the RCA. She is currently working with MacCormac Jamieson Prichard Architects in London and is a visiting lecturer at Brighton University. Her Blood Sense project was shortlisted for the Helen Hamlyn Award and received the runner-up prize for the NGT Creative Thinking for a Responsible Future Award.

Jane Rendell is an architectural designer and historian, art critic and writer, and reader in architecture and art and a director of architectural research at the Bartlett. She is author of *The Pursuit of Pleasure* (Continuum, 2002), and *Art and Architecture* (IB Tauris & Co, 2006), and co-editor of a number of books including *Gender, Space, Architecture* (Spon Press, 1999).

Dagmar Richter is the principal of DR_D Lab, founded in 2000. Her work has been extensively exhibited and published. She is currently a professor at UCLA after teaching at the Art Academy Stuttgart and Berlin-Weissensee, Columbia, RISD, Cooper Union and Harvard.

Sonia Sarkissian is an architect-engineer who has practised architecture in both New York and Athens,

reaching the level of project manager. With a specialism in the design of private residences and furniture, she is also currently completing her PhD (by-practice) in the RCA department of textiles.

Martin Self is a structural engineer with particular interest in innovative structures, geometric complexities and their application in architecture. He joined Arup's Advanced Geometry Unit in 2002, bringing with him knowledge of a range of analysis methods and geometric modelling techniques. He has worked on a wide range of international building and bridge projects.

Tristan Simmonds works as a specialist engineer and designer for Arup within the Advanced Geometry Unit. His expertise lies in the design of lightweight tensile structures, nonlinear analysis, 3-D computational geometry, computer graphics programming and real-time simulation.

Lars Spuybroek is the principal of the NOX architecture office in Rotterdam. He received international recognition after building the Water Pavilion in 1997, and in 2004 the practice finished the D-Tower, Son-O-House and a cluster of cultural buildings in Lille, France (Maison Folies). The 400-page monograph, *NOX: Machining Architecture* was published the same year. He has won several prizes and has exhibited all over the world.

Stefanie Surjo graduated from the Bartlett. During her studies, she gained a commendation on her Diploma thesis 'Living Surface/Habitable skin'. She is now working at Cornish Architects in London.

Peter Testa is widely recognised as an innovator in the tectonics of advanced composite materials for architecture. He is founding director of the Emergent Design Group at MIT, and design principal at Testa & Weiser in Los Angeles where he leads a wide range of projects including Carbon Tower (with Arup).

Jeremy Till and **Sarah Wigglesworth** are directors of Sarah Wigglesworth Architects, best known for the Stock Orchard Street project. Both are professors of architecture at the University of Sheffield where they run the PhD by Design programme. Previous writings include *Architecture and Participation* (Routledge, 2005). They were appointed to curate the British Pavilion at the 2006 Venice Architecture Biennale.

Anne Toomey is the deputy head of the textiles department at the RCA. She is a printed textiles specialist, and her current research focuses on the impact and aesthetic possibilities of new materials and technologies. She co-founded the Architextiles design teaching, learning and research project at the RCA with Mark Garcia in 2004.

Maria Ludovica Tramontin collaborated at NOX until 2004, and is co-founder of the engineering firm Ingenia. She has assisted Lars Spuybroek at the University of Kassel in Germany, at Columbia University and ESARQ, and recently authored *NOX* (Edil Stampa/Ance, 2006).

David Wakefield joined Buro Happold in 1978, where he developed the Happold lightweight structures software, which he has applied to a wide variety of projects. In 1990 he founded Tensys, consulting engineers specialising in the design and analysis of architectural fabric structures, with offices in Bath and Melbourne.

Victoria Watson studied architecture at the Bartlett and at the Polytechnic of Central London. She is the director of The Big Air World, an association formed to develop and promote the phenomenon of the Air Grid. She is a senior lecturer in architecture at the University of Westminster and a partner in the architectural practice Madge & Watson.

Devyn Weiser is design principal of Los Angeles-based Testa & Weiser and co-founder of the Emergent Design Group at MIT. Her work ranges from fashion and product design to large-scale architecture, including the robotically fabricated Strand Tower.

C O N T E N T S

The Hotel of Reflections

Howard Watson describes the derelict 19th-century alcohol factory on the Asian bank of the Bosphorus in Istanbul, which became a 30-year restoration and renovation project for architects Nedret and Mark Butler. On the hotel's completion, their daughter Yasha realised an ingenious treatment of the interiors that takes its cue from the buildings' waterside setting.

The successful modern city is typified by speed, communication and transportation, by the ceaseless blur of multicoloured tracers marking out automatist 'progress' on a time-lapse video. Yet Istanbul is a city of water. Its identity arises out of the romantic, unsubdued and troublesome expanses of the Golden Horn, the Sea of Marmara and the Bosphorus, which lie at its heart and divide up the sprawling city into distinct landmasses across two continents – Europe and Asia.

The Bosphorus is particularly important to the history of the city. The rulers and notables of the Ottoman Empire would spend the summer in their *yalis*, great wooden summerhouses set on the water's edge, where one imagines them contemplating the future of the empire as they looked across the water. The buildings that lie on the shore, many long in ruins, are returning as a focal point for the city's future. Istanbul, famously situated at the axis of East and West, is re-emerging as one of the world's great tourist destinations and the distinctive old buildings of the Bosphorus are being redeveloped into luxury hotels.

On the European side of the water, Les Ottomans, one of the most expensive hotel developments imaginable, sees a pasha's *yali* being converted into a 10-suite hotel at a reported cost of $55 million. Famed Turkish interior designer Zeynep Fadillioglu and experts who worked on restoring Istanbul's Dolmabahce Palace have exuberantly interpreted the Ottoman baroque style, when the empire looked to France for ostentatious decoration. However, immediately opposite, on the Asian side of the city, lies a much smaller, far less expensive yet no less interesting hotel that simultaneously delves into Istanbul's past and looks to the future.

The Sumahan on the Water, developed from a 19th-century former alcohol factory that lay in ruins right on the lip of the Bosphorus, is a 30-year labour of love by a Turkish-American architect couple, Nedret and Mark Butler. In many ways, the drawn-out administrative nightmare the Butlers faced encapsulates the city's difficulties in waking up to its past while bracing itself for an increasingly westward-looking future, but the design itself shows how those concerns can work hand in hand with a great deal of grace.

In 1971, while researching material for her architectural thesis at the University of Minnesota, Nedret realised that her family owned the factory buildings. The Butlers came to work as architects in Istanbul in 1976, and now have a range of successful leisure and residential projects to their name, but all the while have been trying to establish ownership of the former factory buildings and negotiate their future use and design with various planning and historical preservation bodies. One of the benefits of the delay was that their own daughter, Yasha Butler, a ceramist and designer, was by then old enough to look after the interiors.

The result is a subtle architectural feat in which five linked buildings have been either restored or rebuilt to exacting historical standards but house an 18-room hotel in which every single room looks onto the Bosphorus through tall windows. Despite the ordered, historical facade, each room is individually designed with a very contemporary feel. Yet even

Mark Butler, Nedret Butler and Yasha Butler, Sumahan on the Water, Istanbul, 2005–07
Above: The restored and rebuilt, 19th-century facade of the former factory faces the Bosphorus. The hotel's café-bar, furnished with Gloster chairs and tables, reaches out to the waterside, while guests in the duplex loft-suites can step directly into the garden and recline on Adirondack chairs.
Opposite: The hotel was formerly an alcohol factory (fittingly, Sumahan translates as the 'inn of unadulterated spirit'), and the architects have continued links to its industrial past with the use of exposed stonework and black-painted steel girders throughout. The glass lift-shaft espouses the water-linked theme of the design.

Each suite is individually designed and named after a local village. The red Kandilli suite, with its bed built up on a mahogany dais for a view of the water, is a favourite with honeymooners.

Evoking the hammams of the sultans, the bathrooms are grey Marmara marble, with smooth, rounded basins apparently hollowed out from the counter. Kaldewei baths, locally sourced ceramic pendant lights, and internal windows providing views of the Bosphorus offer touches of contemporary luxury.

The library features Mario Bellini's Le Bambole sofa and Vol au Vent chair, Jeffrey Bernett's red Metropolitan armchairs and Antonio Citterio's Apta Collection chair and ottoman.

when Sumahan's contemporary demeanour appears most ardent, it is still rooted in its historical and geographical context. The design is inspired by the flow and transparency of water: the corridors flow directly through the joining seams of the series of buildings; the shades of the Bosphorus, its range of blues, greens and greys, provide the palette for the furnishings; and the lift is a monumental transparent shaft around which the communal areas congregate. An original, single-storey-high stone wall, inlaid with brick patterns and probably built by Greek craftsmen, has been extended up the height of the building and is replicated as a natural, undressed, interior feature throughout the hotel.

Kicking against current trends in the contemporary luxury-hotel market, the Butlers are not scared of darkness, encasing the internal corridor on one level in dark brick, and another in black steel, which is suggestive of the strata of the steep hillside the hotel rests against. The industrial feel of the buildings is maintained through the presence of black steel girders throughout the design. In the guest rooms, square fireplaces, often cut right through semipartition walls, are sometimes given obvious, industrial-looking black flues. In addition to the stone walls, brickwork and black steel, basalt flooring and wooden boards help to create a backdrop of warmth rather than clinical minimalism.

The white-walled reception area, where the black steel rafters are most striking, resolves into a comfortable library furnished with wooden shelving, classics from B&B Italia, and Antonio Citterio's 9750 Apta chair. Unusual, handmade, Ethnicon patchwork kilims feature here as well as throughout the guest rooms. These also include other twists on traditional Turkish designs, with the usually highly patterned tray-top tables here presented as simple, polished silver discs. Hammam-style bathrooms are clad in the grey Marmara marble that was used in the hammams of the sultans' palaces, but large internal windows allow bathers to look out across the room and over the Bosphorus. Many of the suites are in duplex formation, with the bed raised on a platform for further views of the water.

The positioning of all views and services towards the water at the Sumahan makes the hotel a peaceful, contemplative place that undoubtedly re-evokes the intentions of the pashas when they built their summer homes along these shores. ⚙+

Howard Watson is a London-based writer and editor. He is the author of *Hotel Revolution: 21st-Century Hotel Design* (2005), *Bar Style: Hotels and Members' Clubs* (2005) and *The Design Mix: Bars, Cocktails & Style* (2006), all published by John Wiley & Sons.

Icons of Turkish culture – the kilim rug, the ottoman and the large circular tray – are reinterpreted to suit the contemporary luxury-hotel style. Almost all the guest-room furniture has been designed by the Butlers, including Yasha's distinctive floor-lamp stand made up of a string of blown-glass bubbles. The ceiling is in the barrel-vaulted style of the original factory.

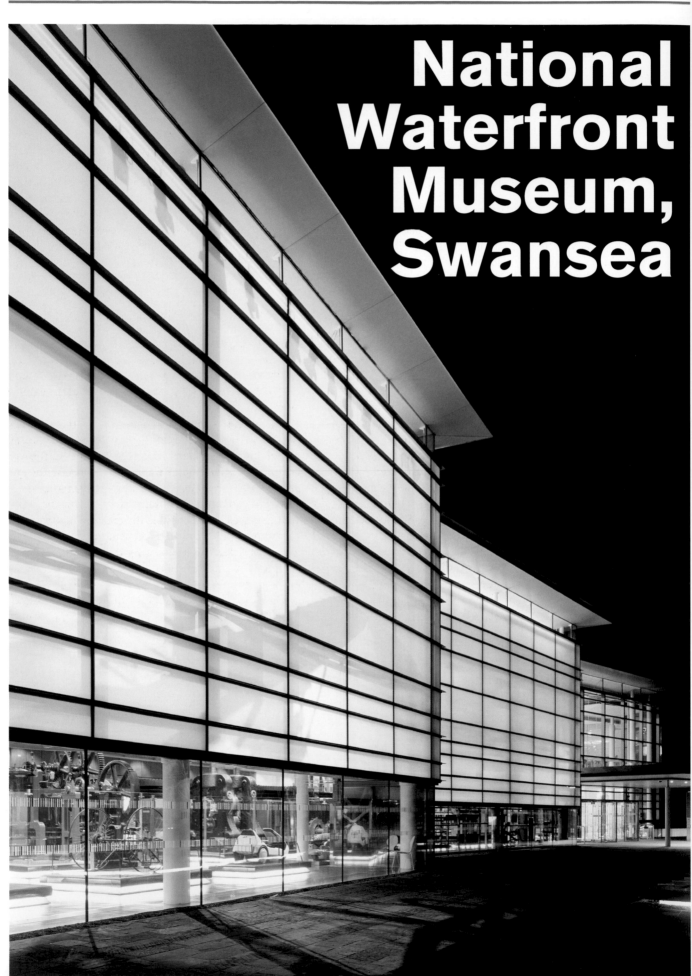

National Waterfront Museum, Swansea

At the National Waterfront Museum in Swansea, Wales, Wilkinson Eyre Architects has united old and new structures, as well as maritime and industrial history. **Jeremy Melvin** describes the curatorial drive behind the museum's construction, and also how the architects have deftly drawn on their own experience of projects that have some association with industry and science.

'One of our ambitions,' says Dr Richard Bevins, keeper of collections services for the National Museum of Wales, the body which operates the National Waterfront Museum, 'was to win European Museum of the Year.' So far the museum has been short-listed for the *Guardian's* Most Family Friendly Visitor Attraction accolade but, having only opened in October 2005, the combination of its design, displays and curatorial goals may yet cause its trophy cabinet to grow. Its design cleverly pulls together elements from its site, its location and its collections to tell the heroic story of Wales's industrial and maritime history.

Somehow, back in the 1970s, when architecture and city planning seemed bent on destroying what life was left in British provincial cities, Swansea made some fundamentally sound decisions. The architecture of its dockland leisure centre may be a poor imitation of the late, lamented Andrew Renton's World Trade Centre on London's St Katherine's Dock, but it did place a hitherto unprovided activity on a site that needed something new. Converting an adjacent dockside warehouse into a museum added to the mix, as did introducing housing, albeit what a design-and-build contractor might have made of Ted Cullinan's blue period housing in London's Leighton Crescent. This lies on the opposite side of the dock, its other side overlooking white sand beaches more commonly associated with the east African coast. Not quite enough, perhaps, to survive the

ineluctable decline of South Wales from an industrial nexus at the heart of an international trading system as commodities, manufacturing and innovative metallurgy have deserted it, but enough to provide a glimmer of hope that the city might have life after post-Scargillite Thatcherism.

Turning this latent potential into a beacon for the future was an underlying aim of the National Museum of Wales's decision to locate its new National Waterfront Museum, one of eight it operates, in the city. The museum's architecture was always intended to be an integral part of its status: 'We wanted an icon,' Bevins recalls, 'something the people of Swansea could be proud of.' The then new National Assembly was thus persuaded to support a procurement strategy based on quality as well as cost, which influenced the decision to appoint Wilkinson Eyre from a short list of six gleaned through an OJEU process. (According to European legislation, all contracts from the public sector that are valued above a certain threshold in going to tender must be published in the *Official Journal of the European Union*.) However, it was the architects' experience in the design of museums and visitor attractions (for example, the Magma Centre in Rotherham and the Science Museum Challenge of Materials Gallery), as well as their clear affinity with industry and the excitement of engineering that gave them the edge.

The architects were appointed towards the end of 2001, some three years after planning for the museum began, and the exhibition designers, Land Design, shortly afterwards. Bevins and his colleagues wanted to reconceive the entire idea of a maritime and industrial museum rather than to be led into an architectural straitjacket. Contingent circumstances made possible the creation of a new institution, while their detailed conceptual work fed into the architects' brief. The previous home for the collection, which is part of the maritime and industrial collections of the National Museum of Wales and is augmented by Swansea's own collection and new material originated, for example, by using IT, was in Cardiff Bay, but visitor numbers were beginning to drop as the age profile increased. And its future

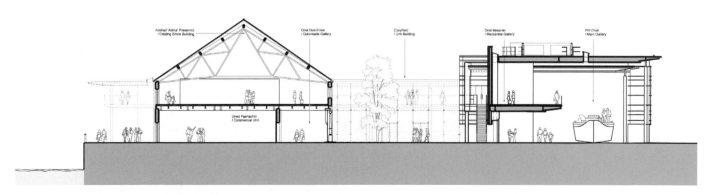

Wilkinson Eyre Architects, National Waterfront Museum, Swansea, Wales, 2004
Above: Section through the old (left) and new galleries. The mezzanine level in the new gallery provides extra interpretive space and an opportunity to look down on the larger exhibits at ground level.
Opposite: At night the low-level strip of clear glass becomes transparent, making the building appear to hover and giving intriguing glimpses into the inside.

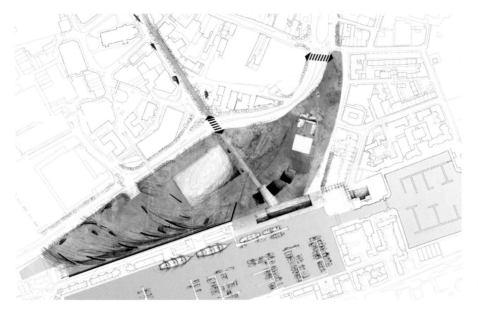

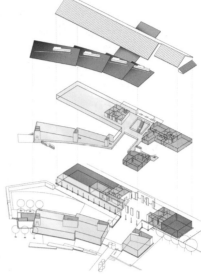

Site masterplan, showing the axis from the city into the building, and the landscaping scheme for the precinct, including the refurbished leisure centre.

Exploded axonometric showing the different elements of new (light blue) and old (dark blue).

was already uncertain when the Development Corporation, heady with the prospect of opera houses and assemblies, made it clear that it would rather have 'festival shopping' on the site. Fortunately they were prepared to pay £7.5 million for it, which meant the museum could buy a factory as a collection centre outside Cardiff for £3 million, with the rest available as matching funding, from the reallocation of existing resources, for the new institution.

Bevins and his colleagues turned this opportunity into a real prospect, recognising that the collection had to be presented differently in order to widen its appeal. Exhibition design and technology would play their part here, but finding the right site that embodied at least some of the subject matter was at least as important. Consequently, all Welsh local authorities were invited to offer possible sites for the new museum; a waterfront location was required as well as some industrial heritage.

Swansea's bid had numerous attractions. The city council offered the maritime and industrial museum it had established in the listed dockside warehouse building, and was also prepared to make a revenue contribution to help offset running costs. The city's industrial heritage credentials were significantly stronger than second-placed Carnaervon, where industry was limited to slate quarrying, compared to Swansea's extraordinary contribution to metallurgy and the tradition of scientific innovation, which kept it at the forefront of metalworking even after the raw materials had to be imported. This in turn tied its maritime and industrial history together, as ships sailed around Cape Horn to bring Chilean copper to play its part in Henry Vivian's machinations, which led to him becoming Lord Swansea in 1893. After tight negotiations regarding the nature and operation of the new museum, all that remained was to

procure the design and sort out funding, which, as is so often the case, were intertwined: to secure £11.1 million – more than a third of the total needed – from the Heritage Lottery Fund, the design needed to be well advanced. Other sources were the Welsh Development Agency, Welsh Tourist Board and the National Assembly, which underwrote the project to the tune of £6 million and provided much needed assistance regarding cash flow.

Wilkinson Eyre specialises in visitor attractions, many of which have some connection to industry and science, often in some combination of their themes, their sites and the existing buildings they appropriate. As a result, the architects have developed an appreciation of narrative: their buildings are not just rhetorical structures, but engage initially with their physical context and increasingly with the thematic content that springs from their function. With its conscious confluence of site and content in a single narrative thread, the National Waterfront Museum is an exemplar of this aspect of the practice's work.

Inherent in the brief was the need for a substantial extension to the warehouse, and Chris Wilkinson quickly recognised that the building would have to face all directions. Northwards is the city centre, south the dock, and on either side local routes and amenities, and this programmatic and practical context meant the building could not have an obvious front and back end. Matching the immediate, local context with the broader urban pattern would bring commercial and accessibility benefits, but could also imply that the story the building told was of a much wider global system – an essential part of the museum's aim is to explain how South Wales was once a global industrial centre. Accordingly, the design takes its axis from Princess Street across the site into a spacious and light entrance foyer,

View of the gallery in the original building showing its magnificent roof.

First- floor plan.

Visitors from the city centre reach the museum via a park.

Ground-floor plan.

through the existing building and via a staircase to a first-floor terrace overlooking the dock. Easy and inviting, this route helps integrate the museum with the city, implying that its message might be relevant to contemporary life. Potentially the route could be open while the rest of the museum is closed, encouraging people to wander to the dock front and bringing custom to the museum's tenant cafés.

The foyer itself is a dramatic space, its character enriched by the axis cutting through at a diagonal, as well as other complex geometries, its potential greatly increased by the lack of pay barriers. It draws entrances from four sides and provides an orientation space, but also, through myriad glazed facets, provides glimpses of the outside, immediate views of other parts of the museum, and more distant ones to the low hills that lie close to the city. Taking advantage of the waterfront on the ground level is a series of shops and cafés, while part of the upper level of the old building, under a splendid roof, has been converted to a gallery space. Interpretive, interactive devices narrate stories that bring life to the collection.

History is visceral in the old building through its fabric. In the new building history is more allusive and this lack of

definitiveness allows it to weave together more threads. Its curving, faceted form derives from the railway lines that once covered the site, and these are further traced in the lines radiating outwards from it. Its cladding is Welsh slate, an important part of the country's industrial heritage. Where the warehouse refers to history through its direct applicability to its original function, in the new building architecture takes this theme further into the imaginative realm. The exhibits here are mainly larger and heavier than those in the older building, with small groups of related objects imaginatively displayed in groups on paternosters, which maximises the number that can be displayed within this relatively small gallery space.

With the onward march of globalisation it is unlikely that South Wales will ever regain its industrial pre-eminence. But the imaginative National Waterfront Museum might help raise awareness of how the area was once at the heart of the early industrialisation that set the pattern for globalisation. Δ+

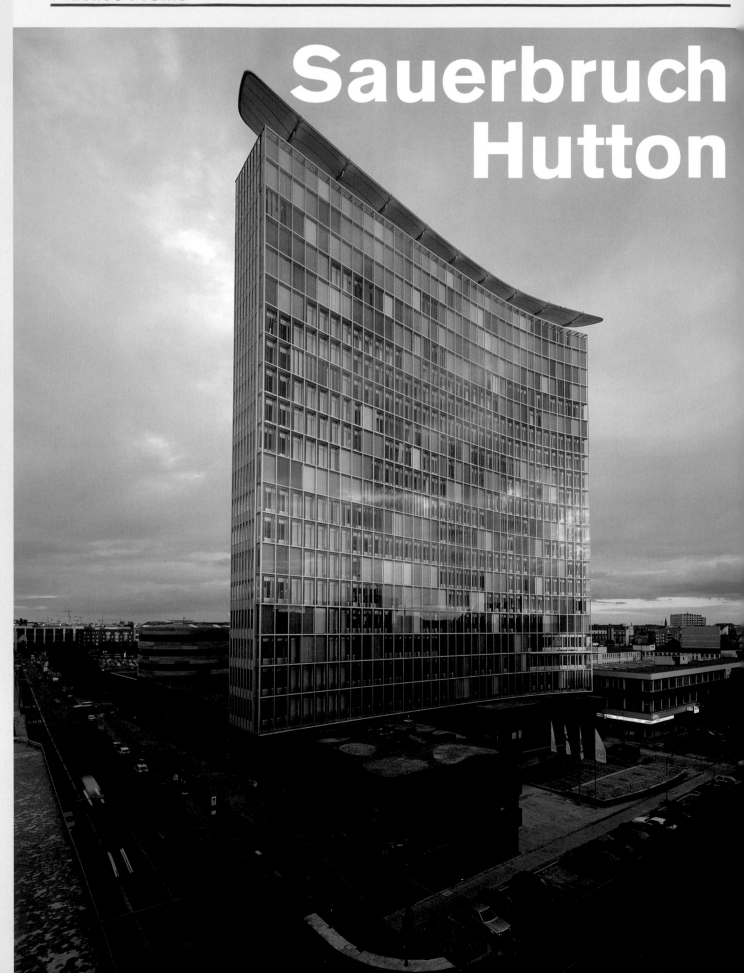

Sauerbruch
Hutton

The bold curves and bright colours in Sauerbruch Hutton's work belie the reasoned, empirical approach they bring to every project. That approach has helped them win numerous competitions, which led to major commissions almost as soon as they opened their office in 1989. **Jayne Merkel** explains how this apparently whimsical architecture grows out of a commitment to existing context, energy conservation and creating a strong sense of place. The sensual experience the buildings provide, inside and out, is always uppermost in the architects' minds.

Nothing about the dark-red-brick, 19th-century army barracks in a semi-industrial area of central Berlin, a mile or so north of the Lehrter station, suggests that the architects at work in the light-filled loft spaces inside might be creating playful-looking, high-tech buildings. But Matthias Sauerbruch and Louisa Hutton, their partners Juan Lucas Young and Jens Ludloff and associates, are designing some of the liveliest and most original architecture in the world today in these very serviceable but rather dour buildings where army uniforms used to be made.

The work may look freewheeling, and it is certainly good humoured, but it is the product of rigorous analysis and conscientious trial and error – an empiricism that the architects attribute to their firm's English roots. Although most of Sauerbruch Hutton's work at this point is in Germany, they were trained at the Architectural Association and began their practice in London, working mainly on small narrow houses where they used colour to visually expand space. Sauerbruch, who is German, had previously worked with Elia Zenghelis at the Office for Metropolitan Architecture (OMA). Hutton, who is English, had worked for Peter and Alison Smithson. The two are married.

In 1990, soon after the Berlin Wall came down, they won a competition to design the GSW housing association's headquarters in the South Friedrichstrasse area that had previously bordered East Berlin. In 1993, they opened their Berlin office, two years later winning another competition there for the Photonic Centre. And in 1998 they were selected to design the Federal Environmental Agency in Dessau in another important competition. The next year they won two more, followed by two more in both 2000 and 2001, and a tenth in 2002. All but one was in Germany, where reunification led to a building boom, the competition system brought commissions to young architects, building technology is very advanced, quality is valued, and clients are unusually open to new ideas.

Sauerbruch Hutton were just the right architects to take advantage of such technological expertise and aesthetic freedom, and their success in competition after competition suggests that their sensuous but responsible approach struck a chord with those in charge of rebuilding.

It was the GSW building that really launched Sauerbruch and Hutton's careers. The tower's gently curved glass facade with continually changing red patterns stands out even in an area where it is surrounded by buildings by Peter Eisenman, Zaha Hadid, John Hejduk, Leon Krier, Daniel Libeskind and Aldo Rossi – and not only because it is taller. It was one of the first double-skinned buildings in Europe, using 40 per cent less energy than was usual at the time of its construction, and the patterns were created by simply installing ordinary pivoting, perforated metal sunshades with the facade. As occupants turn the sunshades at angles, new colour combinations and patterns emerge on the facade. On the ground floor, a dark-grey, three-storey block curves slightly along the street, forming a base for a small green oval structure, and the perpendicular new 20-storey tower. The 16-storey, 1950s high-rise stands adjacent to it. The new tower, which is long and narrow, somewhat obscures the older, almost-square one, but it is intended to visually connect the once-divided parts of Berlin. A thin boomerang-shaped roof hovering over its top helps it make a mark on the horizon.

The GSW Headquarters contained all the essential elements of the architects' later work – colour, shape, an unusual skin, energy efficiency and a quirky way of relating to the urban context. But its innovations seem modest next to the use of shape and colour in the Photonic Centre. Here, for an odd polygonal site in southeast Berlin, the architects designed three multicoloured amoeboid masses (of which two were built) that maintained the scale of nearby buildings but intentionally created something 'discontinuous with the inherited urban fabric' that Sauerbruch saw as 'complete in itself'. The unusual footprints, intended to prove that laboratories do not have to be dull, minimise the space devoted to circulation and maximise that for dark interior labs. Venetian blinds in a spectrum of colours on the facades subtly suggest that the centre was created for the study of light.

Though arrived at rationally, the architects' choices are often provocative. On the edge of the University of Magdeburg, an Experimental Factory merely required a five-storey block of laboratories and offices and a tall, one-storey space for large-scale experiments. But a gigantic orange, pink and silver curved roof drapes over the east and west walls, which are pierced by ribbon windows.

A different kind of wrapper – also curved, but glass, horizontal and irregularly patterned – contains an addition to a red-brick, 19th-century customs house the architects won the

---

GSW Headquarters, Berlin, Germany, 1999
Although this rather high-tech building had the first double facade in Europe, what makes it noticeable on the horizon is its concave facade with patterns created by the sunshades installed within the depth of the facade.

BMW Event and Delivery Centre, Munich, competition entry (first prize), 2001
Amorphous, translucent, multicoloured, multicurved structures under a large, flat, common roof house exhibition halls for events and performances of various kinds at this centre where customers can pick up their cars or be tempted to buy new ones. The three separate buildings are connected by a series of curved drives and ramps so that cars can move through and around the buildings, making the sense of movement suggested by the forms actual as well as visual.

right to convert to a Fire and Police Station for the government district in Berlin in a 1999 competition. The proud Victorian structure, once in a dense area, now stands alone in a quaint, old-fashioned park just across the Spree from the new chancellery, but there are plans for more buildings nearby. The addition, which wraps around the south and east sides of the historic structure, is sheathed in an abstract pattern of red and green glass panels. Although the contrast between the old and restored parts of the building is sharp, somehow each part energises the other and makes a whole.

Daring juxtapositions, curved elements in elevation or plan, unusual colour combinations and energetic patterns are Sauerbruch Hutton's stock in trade, but there is nothing 'stock' about the ways in which they use them. They clad research laboratories for Boehringer Ingelheim Pharma KG in Biberach in a colourful skin of vertical glass louvres arranged in an irregular pattern of reds, ochres and watery greens. In Dogern, where they are building an angular red Innovation and Development Centre with rounded windows for Sedus, an office furniture company, they sheathed a big boxy warehouse in a pattern created by arranging an off-the-shelf cladding system in 20 specially ordered colours.

Curved forms are more common than angular ones in Sauerbruch Hutton's work, but they are almost always used to relate to a landscape context.

In Hennigsdorf, an irregular doughnut-shaped town hall helps connect a small park on the edge of the historical town with a new town centre on the other side of the railway tracks. Four colourful amoeboid office buildings on the Rhine in southern Cologne are intended to relate to their site in the gardens of a 19th-century villa. At the University of Hamburg, three new clustered administration buildings on a triangular site, designed to create a new image for the campus, have

curved ends and colourful, horizontally banded facades. And in Oberhausen, the new Municipal Savings Bank assumes a curved cruciform shape, similar to a starfish, while coloured solar blinds in reflective frames recall glimmering leaves – to make the building itself become a landscape-like form. At the new ADAC Headquarters in Munich, the rounded triangular form of the patterned 16-storey tower mediates between train tracks and city streets, providing an economical plan and creating a recognisable image.

In a winning competition scheme for TV World Hamburg, an 'edutainment park' associated with a television production company, ovals of different sizes contain behind-the-scenes television facilities and amusement areas. Some are surrounded by colourful walls, others by wall-high hedges. Irregular circular forms also predominate at the BMW Event and Delivery Centre in Munich, where three colourful curved volumes are tied together by a large, flat, freeform, transparent overhanging roof. Because cars can enter the interiors and move throughout the entire complex on driveways and ramps, the shapes provide for actual movement and create a sense of movement at the same time.

The undulating forms in the firm's most important building to date, however, the Federal Environmental Agency, were used to turn single-loaded office corridors into a loop that preserves land for a public park, helps mask the size of the building, and forms interior courts overlooked by half the offices. The 400,000-square-metre (4.3-million-square-foot) building is the largest in Dessau, where the German government decided to locate it to stimulate the depressed economy. It not only provides a home for the environmental ministry in a country that takes environmental issues seriously, but also demonstrates how to build responsibly while providing lively, original, exciting spaces for workers and visitors.

Federal Environmental Agency, Dessau, Germany, 2005

In a 1998 international competition, Sauerbruch Hutton was selected to design this building which epitomises the principles the 800 people who work there are charged with implementing. The architects took advantage of the fact that 850 cubic metres (30,000 cubic feet) of earth had to be excavated from the polluted site, installing one of the largest heat-exchange systems available to suck air in from outside, circulate it through the ground, return it to the building, and ventilate it through wall plenums and the winter-garden roof. The building is made of nontoxic, recycled or reusable materials, with considerable thermal insulation and windows that can be opened a little. It incorporates an existing 19th-century railway station structure as well as a former factory that has been refitted to serve as a dense storage area for library books. In terms of energy consumption for heating, the agency uses a quarter of the amount of other government buildings.

The four-storey agency is composed of a 365-metre (1,200-foot) long, narrow, double-loaded corridor lined with offices that look out either on the surrounding park or interior courts. Every office has a unique view. The corridor snakes along the irregular site enclosing courtyards and saving enough land – 30 per cent of the site – to create a public park along one side. The area just inside the entrance, called the Forum, is an enclosed public space with facilities for visitors and access to the shared areas of the building, such as an auditorium and the largest environmental library in Europe. Between horizontal timber bands that bend around the curves, glass panels in 53 different hues create a pattern weighted towards reds near the old brick railway station building, towards blues in the Forum, and towards greens in the open landscape. The building further fits into its setting because one cannot see the whole thing in a single view.

This $82 million complex is a model of sustainable architecture, but as usual in Sauerbruch Hutton's work, aesthetics (appearance, feel, atmosphere) played a major role in every decision. Air shafts to the underground heat-exchanger were designed by artist Hans-Joachim Haertel and appear to be freestanding sculptures. Each one is unique. The oval cafeteria has walls of glass that look out over the surrounding park. Interior courtyards, corridors, even staircases are composed with sensuous curves. And colour creates variety, connections with elements all around, and breaks down the scale of the long wall surfaces. Texture also plays a role, as does, of course, the natural light that filters through the glass roofs of the Forum and the Atrium.

Fire and Police Station, Berlin, 2004

The new facilities were built in and around the red-brick Hauptzollamt Packhof (main customs goods yard) constructed in the 19th century, but the architects made no attempt to have the addition match the original. The curved-glass addition that wraps around the south and east sides of the old building contrasts daringly, the same way new buildings the architects design do with their urban neighbours. Some coloured glass panels flip up to provide natural ventilation. Although the colours – red to symbolise the fire station and green the police – represent the departments that occupy the building, they also recall the various shades of red in the brickwork and the greens in the nearby park on the banks of the Spree.

   Because pedestrian access from a street on the north is now a full storey higher than the land on the south side towards the Spree, where vehicles enter, the architects created a glass-walled footbridge to the building from the sidewalk and a new entrance through what used to be a second-storey window. They used the change in grade to tuck the garage in under the wrapper that contains new spaces for people. On the ground floor, gigantic cruciform concrete columns support the glass-walled offices and meeting rooms above while dividing parking spaces for police cars and fire trucks from one another and allowing emergency vehicles easy access and space for quick exits. Since the side walls of the old customs house are also stucco or concrete, the columns also tie the new and old parts together.

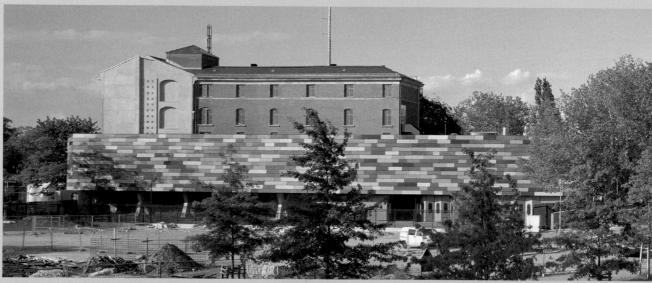

Museum for the Brandhorst Collection, Munich, Germany, due for completion 2008

Because it is located in the museum quarter, near the Alte Pinakothek, the museum has a geometric shape derived from the street plan. The three-storey structure consists of an elongated rectangle with an irregular quadrangular 'head building' at the corner of Theresien and Türkenstrasse, where works by Cy Twombly will be shown. The facade is divided chromatically into three areas that demarcate various types of galleries inside with different qualities of daylight and proportions. Those on the lowest level, with artificial light, to be used for the display of media and graphic art, will surround a large daylit patio. On the ground floor, seven universal galleries will be illuminated by a daylighting system that brings zenith light into the interior through a series of reflectors.

The largest exhibition spaces are on the top floor where they will be naturally lit from above. This dramatic spacious gallery resembles one the architects created in their winning 2001 competition scheme for the still-unbuilt Museum of Contemporary Art and Moving Image Centre in Sydney, Australia, where it was intended to provide new, well-lit space on top of an existing building and a colourful new addition. In Munich, a more restrained skin than the one proposed for Sydney relates to the dignified museum area and prepares visitors for a rarified and intense experience with contemporary art inside.

A generous interior staircase will connect all three floors of galleries, which will be subtly differentiated by quality of light, dimensions and a deliberate variation in sequence. The idea is to create a varied museum experience that approximates the domestic quality of the environment where the collection was amassed. The outside, though dignified enough to fit into the museum quarter, is intended to suggest that this is a place where contemporary, living art can be seen. The building's skin consists of square-profile ceramic batons suspended vertically in front of a horizontally folded rainscreen. The overall effect of the myriad batons will be a uniform appearance from afar, but a contrasting and lively three-dimensional surface nearby. As the surface is articulated in zones of three different tonalities that demarcate the interior structure of the exhibition galleries, the visitor is prepared for the varied experience inside where each part of the collection is shown in an ideal light condition.

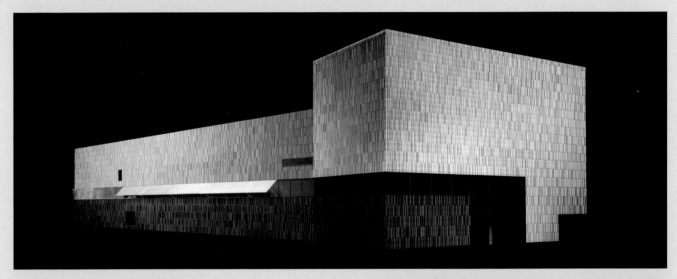

Museum of Contemporary Art and Moving Image Centre, Sydney, competition entry (first prize), 2001
This is the second scheme for the museum on a quay across the water from the Sydney Opera House. The translucent box of galleries on top was initially intended to create light-filled spaces on top of the museum's current home in a 1950s Maritime Services building, and also over a new three-storey bean-shaped movie theatre. The gallery was retained in the second scheme, after the brief changed and the old building was to be demolished, replacing it with another new colourful, plaid-walled structure with rounded ends on one side and clear glass walls overlooking the harbour.

The ministry is located only steps from the railway station on a brownfield site where a gasworks used to be, and is connected to a 19th-century railway station building with which it contrasts as spiritedly as the architects' Fire and Police Station in Berlin does. It snakes along the narrow site between a throughway and the railway tracks. Its entrance on the long side, from the park, leads to a landscaped public 'forum' that serves as a link between the library, information centre, meeting hall and a more private atrium surrounded by interior offices. The canteen is housed in a separate building in the park itself, so employees have to go outside every day – into the environment they are charged with maintaining. The ministry building is made of materials selected for ecological sustainability. Its compact volumes have intensive thermal insulation, and one of the largest heat exchangers currently available recovers heat and cool air from the thermal mass in the ground. And, with its curvaceous forms, warm larch cladding with fire-protective coating on the inner side, and patterned coloured-glass walls, it makes sustainability sexy.

Although most of the buildings under way now also have colourful curved walls, at least one, the Museum for the Brandhorst Collection in Munich, suggests another direction. It is more subdued in its formal language, being mainly

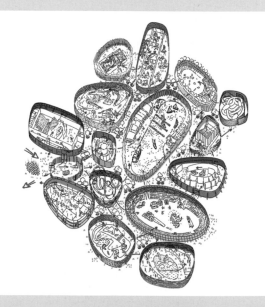

TV World, Hamburg, competition entry (first prize), 2000
The facilities for this 'edutainment park' associated with a television production company are each housed in irregular ovals that seem to float on land like islands on water. Some are surrounded by colourful walls, others by wall-high hedges. Some house rides and game areas, others have theatres and interactive television, but all have the quality of a colourful fantasy land.

rectilinear with a taller trapezoidal 'head' building, which, marking a prominent corner in the museum district forms the entrance to the building. The spaces inside are distinguished by the character and the quality of the light, in each case chosen to optimally illuminate specific works of late 20th-century and contemporary art (mostly paintings), to be shown in each gallery. The long, tall, narrow, skylighted exhibition space on top resembles an almost rectangular, double-height white box that the architects designed for the Museum of Contemporary Art and Moving Image Centre in Sydney, Australia, a winning competition scheme of 2001. That box was intended to create light-filled galleries on top of the museum's current home in a 1950s Maritime Services building, on a quay across the water from the Sydney Opera House, and a new curved three-storey structure for the cinema. And it survived a change in the rules; when competitors were no longer required to keep the old building they simply replaced it with a new one, which was plaid like the bean-shaped theatre.

The Brandhorst Museum, for a very different kind of site, is much more subtle and urbane. It has been designed specifically to accommodate a sophisticated private collection of recent art to which it defers while still trying to 'provoke, surprise, and delight all the senses', as Sauerbruch Hutton's buildings always do. Because the architects' work is so much more than practical, it has been the subject of several successful one-firm exhibitions, including '1234' at the Architekturmuseum der TU-München within the Pinakothek der Moderne in Munich from June through October of this year. So, when the Brandhorst is completed, visitors will know where it fits in the architects' body of continually evolving work. And they will probably come to realise that what seems like whimsy is also uncommonly wise. Δ

Resumé

Sauerbruch Hutton

1989
Sauerbruch Hutton founded in London

1990
GSW Headquarters, Berlin, competition (first prize)

1993
Berlin office opened

1995
Photonic Centre, Berlin, competition (first prize)

1998
Photonics Centre, Berlin, completed
Federal Environmental Agency, Dessau, competition (first prize)

1999
GSW Headquarters Building completed
Fire and Police Station, Berlin, competition (first prize)
University Administration Buildings, Hamburg, competition (first prize)
Zumtobel Staff Showroom, Berlin
'WYSIWYG' (What You See Is What You Get) exhibition, Architectural Association, London

2000
ICE Terminal, Cologne, competition (first prize)
TV World, Hamburg, competition (first prize)
Offices on the Rhine, Cologne, competition (due for completion 2008)
'On the way to Dessau' exhibition, Federal Environmental Agency at Expo 2000, Dessau
New German Headquarters of the British Council, Berlin

2001
Experimental Factory, Magdeburg
BMW Event and Delivery Centre, Munich, competition (first prize)
Museum of Contemporary Art and Moving Image Centre, Sydney, competition (first prize)

2002
Research laboratories for Boehringer Ingelheim Pharma KG, Biberach
Museum for Brandhorst Collection, Munich, competition (first prize), due for completion 2008
Innovation and Development Centre for Sedus, Dogern, competition (warehouse recladding completed 2003, Innovation and Development Centre at design stage)
'Plus' multimedia installation, Kunst-Werke, Berlin

2003
Town Hall, Hennigsdorf
Trade Fair Boulevard, Cologne, competition (first prize)

2004
Fire and Police Station, Berlin, completed
Municipal Savings Bank, Oberhausen, competition (first prize), due for completion 2007/08
ADAC Headquarters, Munich, competition (first prize), due for completion 2009
KFW Banking Group West Arcade, Frankfurt, competition (first prize), due for completion 2008

2005
Federal Environmental Agency, Dessau, completed
'Sense and Sensuality' exhibition, Harvard Graduate School of Design, Cambridge, Massachusetts
Jessop West, Sheffield, competition (first prize), due for completion 2008

2006
'1234: The Architecture of Sauerbruch Hutton' exhibition, Architekturmuseum der TU-München, Pinakothek der Moderne, Munich
St Georges Centre, Geneva
Domus Centre, Frankfurt, competition (first prize)

Louisa Hutton and Matthias Sauerbruch.

Project Units 2b and 2c, Nuovo Portello, Milan

The once industrial area immediately surrounding Milan is undergoing a transformation. **Valentina Croci** describes a sizable development at Nuovo Portello currently being undertaken by the Milanese architect Cino Zucchi, on a site close to the old trade fair. She explains how Zucchi is, in this particularly fragmented urban context, seeking a solution that is 'do-it-yourself city planning on a miniature scale', while also drawing on his considerable practical and academic knowledge of Milanese housing design.

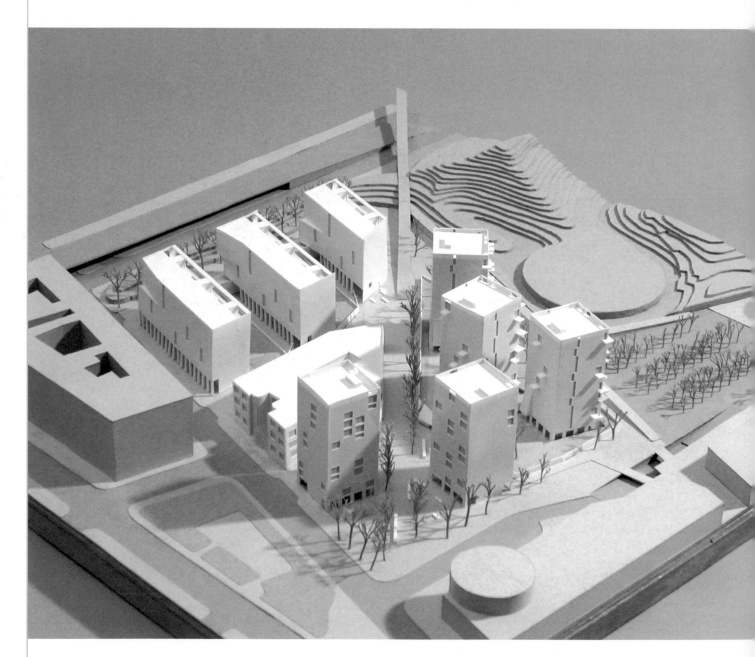

The proposal for a private and subsidised residential complex by Cino Zucchi Architetti (CZA) at Nuovo Portello, close to the former trade fair site to the northwest of the Milan, is part of a series of projects for the abandoned industrial areas on the outskirts of the city. Its comprehensive plan, like that for the residential development of the former trade fair area,[1] is a response to the increasing demand for service-sector and residential spaces, and the integrated development of public- (for example, green spaces, a new transportation system, and new administrative buildings) and private-sector services.

Other parts of the city undergoing extensive regeneration include the ring area to the north. Taken over by industrial groups after the Second World War, and by hulking residential buildings during the great urban development of the 1960s and 1970s, this area is now taking on a new form through projects such as that for the new Navigli area (including the conversion of a former hospital for residential use), the large complex at Porta Vittoria with a new library by Bolles & Wilson, and major work in the Garibaldi-Repubblica area[2] (which will serve to reconnect noncohesive areas cut off by the series of railway lines in and out of the nearby Garibaldi train station).

In addition to CZA's residential buildings on Viale Serra, the main sites being developed in Nuovo Portello, according to a masterplan by Studio Valle Architetti Associati, are a shopping centre by Studio Valle (already completed), a park by Andreas Kipar/Land srl and Charles Jencks (under construction), a square with service-sector and commercial buildings also by Studio Valle, and a housing complex by Canali Associati (work on the latter two projects has yet to begin). The area also includes the former Alfa Romeo facilities, the highly controversial conversion of which even involved an unsuccessful foray by Aldo Rossi. The former Alfa Romeo cafeteria building on Via Traiano forms part of CZA's residential project.

Nuovo Portello is severed by a diagonal axis from the CZA apartments to the Studio Valle square, passing over the Viale Serra via a footbridge. This axis is the unifying element of the sites (though not including the shopping centre), as well as the compositional basis of CZA's proposal. The orientation of Zucchi's buildings is based on maximum exposure to sunlight, but more importantly to shield the apartments from noise from, and views of, the busy Viale Serra.

The complex includes three eight-storey horizontal blocks and two corner towers which will provide subsidised housing, and three private, mixed-use towers. The horizontal blocks are set in a row, with the two corner towers dominating Via Traiano and defining entrances to Kipar and Jencks' natural park with its mixture of public and private spaces. Here, the

Entrance to the complex from the diagonal axis that crosses the entire Nuovo Portello according to Studio Valle's masterplan. The tall buildings are not conceived as isolated towers. Rather they are a 'porous' passage from the rigid grid of the city to the fluid forms of the park designed by Andreas Kipar/Land srl and Charles Jencks. Cladding materials for the facades of the three mixed-use towers are of various-coloured stone, wood and aluminium.

high density of homes contrasts with the expansive green space of the park, as in some of the best architecture in Milan; for example, Lodovico Magistretti's tower in Sempione Park (1920) and the buildings by Luigi Caccia Dominioni in the nearby neighbourhood of Pagano (1913), both of which include horizontal blocks and towers arranged in a courtyard-type pattern, fraying towards the green areas – a model Zucchi adopted for his Nuovo Portello project.

Such examples of local architecture are familiar to Zucchi, who was born in Milan, graduated there, and now lives in the city. Furthermore, his practice has much experience in designing residential and public spaces within stratified urban areas, an excellent example of which is its masterplan for the large abandoned area of the former Junghans factory on Giudecca Island in Venice, for which the practice also designed five new buildings that are now either completed or under construction.

The scale of CZA's project at Nuovo Portello lies between that of a neighbourhood plan and a single building designed and isolated from its context. Though the complex is not in itself urban planning, it relates to the overall urban plan in its use of some of the formal components of public spaces: porticoes, basements, visual perspectives and symmetries.[3] Likewise, the concave, rather than convex, orientation of the two corner towers, from which the diagonal axis emanates, emphasises the semipublic nature of the site and creates an urban permeability without closing off the units as in a gated community.

This building scale is typical of architectures built in empty spaces in historic cities as part of their functional

---

Cino Zucchi Architetti, Project Units 2b and 2c, Nuovo Portello, Milan, due for completion end 2006
The complex includes three eight-storey horizontal blocks and two corner towers that will provide subsidised housing, and three private, mixed-use towers. The Via Traiano side includes the former Alfa Romeo cafeteria, which was turned into offices and a fitness centre as part of the project, with an outdoor café facing the new square inside the complex.

McLean's Nuggets

Sounds Good

Acoustics and, more specifically, the acoustics of the concert venue remain a dark art. The Royal Festival Hall in London (the sole physical legacy of the 1951 Festival of Britain, a 'tonic to the nation') was not retained because of an excellent acoustic characteristic, but as a well-serviced public building in a nascent art park (see cloakrooms, WCs, bars, etc). Sir Simon Rattle was certainly talking about the acoustics when he described the Festival Hall as 'the worst major concert arena in Europe'. Currently being refurbished for the not inconsiderable sum of £70 million (with the assistance of Larry Kirkegaard of Chicago-based acoustic consultants Kirkegaard Associates), why has London not sought to create new venues of venerable acoustic timbre? Pioneering acoustician and accomplished jazz musician Sandy Brown proposed exactly this in July 1970 with his Phonodrome project, a 'purely electronic amphitheatre' to seat around 10,000 people. Brown objected to the almost puritanical distaste '... from the prestigious musical establishment figures ... that any kind of electronics means an adulterated and therefore degraded sound message', and added that musicians had been unable to tell whether or not the assisted 'Helmholtz' resonance system retrofitted in the Festival Hall was switched on or off during testing. Brown's much larger venue (the Royal Festival Hall only has a capacity of 3,000) would answer the economic problem of subsidising an orchestra while attempting to use the currently available technology for good acoustic propagation. Who knows whether this would have been an aesthetic or electroacoustic success – and does it matter? If we are not willing to take a chance on new methods of semipurposeful time-wasting then where does that leave us other than in the antique trade? Brown's communiqué also makes mention of Michael Gerzon, whose work with the 'directional psychoacoustics' of

Ambisonics for the recording and commercial reproduction of domestic surround sound was then being supported by the National Research Development Corporation; unfortunately his untimely death, aged 50, in 1996 may have robbed us of a more ubiquitous three-dimensional sonic world.

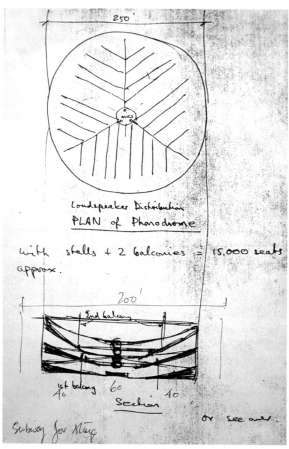

Sandy Brown, Sketch of the Phonodrome, 1970.

Corporate Creativity

There appears to be a current clamour for all things creative and for defining and co-opting the mythical realm of creativity, the creative act and the creative singular being. A three-page advertorial in the *New York Times* (20 April 2006) tells us that corporate-computing behemoth IBM, in collaboration with other similarly sized companies such as General Electric (GE) and eBay, is 'thinking out of the box', or some such linguistic delusion, and welcomes us to the 'innovation era'. Oil and waste companies in the UK have also been taking full-page advertisements celebrating their environmental epiphany and commitment to the inventive

potential of future generations. In her recently published book *The Creating Brain: The Neuroscience of Genius*, Nancy C Andreasen attempts to define the essential characteristics of creativity, describing the seemingly contradictory qualities of the creative person, which include adventure and sensitivity, ambiguity and persistence. If the 'creative' is difficult to define, then creating an environment within which an artist can work is another mechanism to release or nurture some kind of creative act. These places should be the state-funded schools, but remain as a handful of idiosyncratic organisations that may have limited life spans – see the much-documented Black Mountain College (1933–56), whose alumni include composer John Cage, choreographer Merce Cunningham and Tensegrity pioneer Kenneth Snelson. An article in the *Wall Street Journal* (20 March 2006) entitled 'Nurturing Innovation' detailed ways in which businesses and their employees could be more creative. It featured a description of the working pattern of the MacDowell Colony in New Hampshire, which has provided free eight-week fellowships since 1907. Composers such as Aaron Copland and Jason Eckart have enjoyed uninterrupted beatific seclusion in one of 32 cabins, equipped with the required tools of the specific artist and few social/dietary obligations. The article also quotes Richard Florida, the author of *The Rise of The Creative Class*, who says that in future a successful company 'will look more like an artist colony or inventor's laboratory than the office of today'. Governments take note, although no government is good at creative – and certainly not this dog-day UK administration over which still hangs the sour whiff of half-baked sponsored patronage in North Greenwich. For genuine creativity read freedom, good servicing (be that practical or social) and trust. Good servicing at a governmental level is a fine-tuned civil service, and for freedom and trust put the responsibility for good art in the hands of artists not administrators.

Invisible University faculty meeting, Regents Park, 2005.

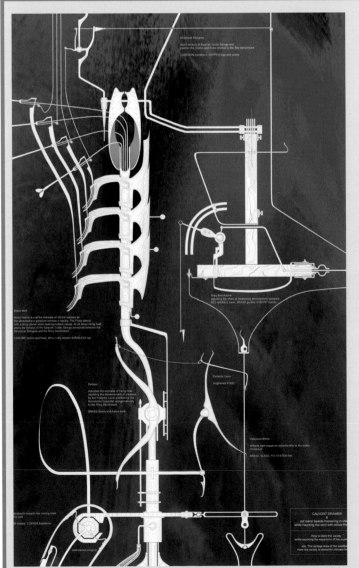
Detail of Calycist Drawer, from Alex Schramm's organic engine garden, 2006.

Stirling Works

If technology enables us to rightly revisit the speculative ideas of futurologists such as Francis Bacon and Richard Buckminster Fuller, then it is only logical that we revisit the unexploited associated technologies of former generations that may have suffered from misappropriation, misunderstanding, 'wrong-purposing' or indifference. A good example of this reinvention is the Stirling engine. Invented by Ayrshire clergyman Reverend Robert Stirling in 1816 as the 'Economiser', a Stirling engine employs a piston and cylinder mechanism with a fixed body of gas such as air or helium, externally heated and cooled to expand and contract, converting temperature differential into physical movement. Because of the separated fuel source it has also been called an 'external' combustion engine. A Stirling engine can be powered by almost any kind of fuel and has remained an emblematic curio for the environmental technologist, with only limited commercial application until now. Stirling Energy Systems (SES) is utilising 12,000 Stirling engines over 7.7 square kilometres (3 square miles) in a planned 900-megawatt (the equivalent of two gas-fired power stations) solar-thermal system in Imperial Valley, southern California. The engines are mounted at the focal point of a solar tracking mirror array and run almost silently with little or no maintenance required. Another enthusiastic champion of the Stirling engine is Segway® inventor Dean Kamen who, with his research company DEKA, is currently developing his own version. The Segway® Human Transporter (HT) was originally rumoured to be powered by such an engine. *Δ*+

'McLean's Nuggets' is an ongoing technical series inspired by Will McLean and Samantha Hardingham's enthusiasm for back issues of *AD*, as explicitly explored in Hardingham's *AD* issue *The 1970s is Here and Now* (March/April 2005). Will McLean is joint coordinator (with Pete Silver) of technical studies in the Department of Architecture at the University of Westminster. He is currently on sabbatical working with Adam Kalkin on his Quik House project in New Jersey, US.

Fiat Tagliero Service Station

In 2006, the spotlight has very much been on the Modern Movement, with the major exhibition at the V&A in London – 'Modernism: Designing a New World 1914–1936'. Here, Edward Denison describes how Giuseppe Pettazzi's Fiat Tagliero service station in Asmara in Eritrea, East Africa, epitomised Italy's futuristic ambitions for a new colony.

In 1935, aeroplanes of the Italian air force rained hell in the Horn of Africa, massacring unarmed civilians with chemical shells that set 'a precedent for Mussolini's son to exult sadistically over the thrills of chasing native spearmen across the plains of Ethiopia in his fighter-bomber and to write glowingly of the glorious sunburst of exploding bombs'.[1] The assault was launched from Eritrea, Italy's first colonial foothold in Africa and home to Italy's revered colonial settlement, Asmara, a relatively sleepy town before Mussolini embarked on his dream of realising Italy's East African empire.

Having begun colonising Eritrea in 1885, Italy consolidated its position in 1935 with the influx of nearly 70,000 civilians and military personnel. With this, Asmara experienced an unprecedented construction boom that lasted until Italy's surrender in 1941. As the Eritrean capital burgeoned under the gains of a false war economy, one of the world's most complete Modernist cities was built. In just six years, the humble town perched on the edge of Africa's northeastern highlands was transformed into the continent's most modern

city, with more traffic lights than Rome, a road network that spread out as far as Sudan, southern Ethiopia and Somalia, and more than 50,000 motorcars.

Representing modernity, physically and figuratively, this nascent mode of transport offered many new and exciting design opportunities. In Eritrea, Italian architects and engineers, less constrained by domestic professional regulations, allowed their imaginations to run wild, designing and constructing a wide range of flamboyant structures. Nowhere else in the country, or the entire continent, was this exemplified more than in the design of Asmara's Fiat Tagliero service station constructed in 1938. Located outside the city centre at the junction of the two main southbound roads, one leading to the new airport and the other to Ethiopia, the futuristic form of Fiat Tagliero soars above the road, imitating what was the most explicit symbol of modernity at the time – the aeroplane.

The two-storey main body containing offices and the service counter echoes a cockpit with sleek wraparound windows. Above this soars an ornamental tower, its erectness accentuated by the vertical lines of the window frames, the cockpit's bull-nosed frontage and the two flagpoles crowning the building. More impressive and far more audacious are its 30-metre (98-foot) cantilevered reinforced concrete wings that hang from the structure with breathtaking weightlessness. The unreserved impressiveness of this volant structure is most conspicuous when standing beneath the building's massive wings, the sky forming an appropriate backdrop under the canopy of what surely ranks among the most astounding futuristic structures in Africa.

The temerarious design stunned the municipal authorities who, disbelieving of architect Giuseppe Pettazzi's calculations, insisted that supporting columns be included in the final design. This myth proved fact when the original plans were recently unearthed, showing each wing being propped up by 15 poles. The compromise doubtless irked the building's architect, who saw his bold design unceremoniously rooted to the floor and appearing unfinished. Unbowed by the bureaucratic setback, he constructed his aeroplane with its wings supported by wooden pillars. According to urban legend,

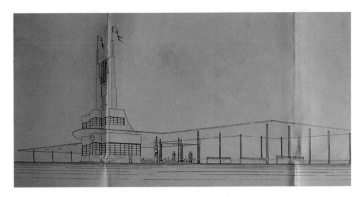

The architect's drawings showing the supporting poles to ensure its approval by the municipal authorities.

at the building's unveiling the architect put a gun to the contractor's head and ordered him to remove the supports. Under duress, the builder duly complied with Pettazzi's demands. When the supports were taken away, the wings stayed aloft and have remained that way for seven decades.

It is heartening, too, that the wings are likely to last at least another seven decades, since the service station has recently undergone a major renovation as part of Eritrea's undertaking to preserve and promote its architectural heritage worldwide. This it views as an international legacy, and which the building's owner and the country's Cultural Assets Rehabilitation Project should be applauded for their commitment. It is hoped that Asmara will receive UNESCO World Heritage status in the near future, as Eritrea, Africa's youngest country and one of the poorest in the world, aims to invite international appeal and encourage development through the careful promotion of its cultural heritage assets.

Fascist-era buildings are not legacies immediately evocative of reflective pining that call for preservation. However, architecture, being the physical manifestation of history, represents the fortunes of a location and creates a sense of place – a characteristic for which Asmara has been internationally acknowledged. Although the rightful proprietors of Asmara have adopted a city designed under an odious regime, Eritreans are deeply proud of what they have made of their capital, and that it was built by an Eritrean workforce. Today, Asmara is one of Africa's most charming urban environments. In a region of Africa where aeroplanes once delivered destruction, another aeroplane has become the symbol of a city's attempt to revive itself through its architectural heritage – a built heritage that ranks among the most remarkable in the world. ⌂+

Edward Denison is an independent writer, consultant and photographer based in the UK and China. He has worked with various international organisations and presents regularly at symposia around the world. He is co-author with Guang Yu Ren of *Building Shanghai: The Story of China's Gateway* (John Wiley & Sons, 2006) and *Asmara: Africa's Secret Modernist City* (Merrell, 2003 and 2007).

Note
1 P Finch, *Shanghai and Beyond*, Charles Scribner's Sons (New York), 1953, p 245.

Giuseppe Pettazzi, Fiat Tagliero service station, Asmara, Eritrea, 1938
Above: This impressive, recently renovated building will be converted into a café.
Opposite: The futuristic Fiat Tagliero service station before being renovated in 2004.

Subscribe Now

As an influential and prestigious architectural publication, *Architectural Design* has an almost unrivalled reputation worldwide. Published bimonthly, it successfully combines the currency and topicality of a newsstand journal with the editorial rigour and design qualities of a book. Consistently at the forefront of cultural thought and design since the 1960s, it has time and again proved provocative and inspirational – inspiring theoretical, creative and technological advances. Prominent in the 1980s and 1990s for the part it played in Postmodernism and then in Deconstruction, in the 2000s ⌀ has leveraged a depth and level of scrutiny not currently offered elsewhere in the design press. Topics pursued question the outcomes of technical innovations as well as the far-reaching social, cultural and environmental challenges that present themselves today in a period of increasing global uncertainty. ⌀

SUBSCRIPTION RATES 2007
Institutional Rate (Print only
or Online only): UK£175/US$315
Institutional Rate (Combined Print
and Online): UK£193/US$347
Personal Rate (Print only):
UK £110/US$170
Discount Student* Rate
(Print only): UK£70/US$110

*Proof of studentship will be required when placing an order. Prices reflect rates for a 2007 subscription and are subject to change without notice.

TO SUBSCRIBE
Phone your credit card order:
+44 (0)1243 843 828

Fax your credit card order to:
+44 (0)1243 770 432

Email your credit card order to:
cs-journals@wiley.co.uk

Post your credit card or
cheque order to:
John Wiley & Sons Ltd.
Journals Administration Department
1 Oldlands Way
Bognor Regis
West Sussex PO22 9SA
UK

Please include your postal
delivery address with your order.

All ⌀ volumes are available individually.
To place an order please write to:
John Wiley & Sons Ltd
Customer Services
1 Oldlands Way
Bognor Regis
West Sussex PO22 9SA

Please quote the ISBN number of the issue(s) you are ordering.

⌀ is available to purchase on both a subscription basis and as individual volumes

○ I wish to subscribe to ⌀ *Architectural Design* at the **Institutional rate of (Print only or Online only** *(delete as applicable)* **£175/US$315.**

○ I wish to subscribe to ⌀ *Architectural Design* at the **Institutional rate of (Combined Print and Online) £193/US$347.**

○ I wish to subscribe to ⌀ *Architectural Design* at the **Personal rate of £110/US$170.**

○ I wish to subscribe to ⌀ *Architectural Design* at the **Student rate of £70/US$110.**

○ ⌀ *Architectural Design* is available to individuals on either a calendar year or rolling annual basis; Institutional subscriptions are only available on a calendar year basis. Tick this box if you would like your Personal or Student subscription on a rolling annual basis.

Payment enclosed by Cheque/Money order/Drafts.

Value/Currency £/US$ ☐

○ Please charge £/US$ ☐
to my credit card.
Account number:

☐☐☐☐ ☐☐☐☐ ☐☐☐☐ ☐☐☐☐

Expiry date:

☐☐☐☐

Card: Visa/Amex/Mastercard/Eurocard *(delete as applicable)*

Cardholder's signature ☐

Cardholder's name ☐

Address ☐

☐

☐ Post/Zip Code ☐

Recipient's name ☐

Address ☐

☐

☐ Post/Zip Code ☐

I would like to buy the following issues at £22.99 each:

○ ⌀ 184 *Architextiles*, Mark Garcia

○ ⌀ 183 *Collective Intelligence in Design*, Christopher Hight + Chris Perry

○ ⌀ 182 *Programming Cultures: Art and Architecture in the Age of Software*, Mike Silver

○ ⌀ 181 *The New Europe*, Valentina Croci

○ ⌀ 180 *Techniques and Technologies in Morphogenetic Design*, Michael Hensel, Achim Menges + Michael Weinstock

○ ⌀ 179 *Manmade Modular Megastructures*, Ian Abley + Jonathan Schwinge

○ ⌀ 178 *Sensing the 21st-Century City*, Brian McGrath + Grahame Shane

○ ⌀ 177 *The New Mix*, Sara Caples and Everardo Jefferson

○ ⌀ 176 *Design Through Making*, Bob Sheil

○ ⌀ 175 *Food + The City*, Karen A Franck

○ ⌀ 174 *The 1970s Is Here and Now*, Samantha Hardingham

○ ⌀ 173 *4dspace: Interactive Architecture*, Lucy Bullivant

○ ⌀ 172 *Islam + Architecture*, Sabiha Foster

○ ⌀ 171 *Back To School*, Michael Chadwick

○ ⌀ 170 *The Challenge of Suburbia*, Ilka + Andreas Ruby

○ ⌀ 169 *Emergence*, Michael Hensel, Achim Menges + Michael Weinstock

○ ⌀ 168 *Extreme Sites*, Deborah Gans + Claire Weisz

○ ⌀ 167 *Property Development*, David Sokol

○ ⌀ 166 *Club Culture*, Eleanor Curtis

○ ⌀ 165 *Urban Flashes Asia*, Nicholas Boyarsky + Peter Lang

○ ⌀ 164 *Home Front: New Developments in Housing*, Lucy Bullivant

○ ⌀ 163 *Art + Architecture*, Ivan Margolius

○ ⌀ 162 *Surface Consciousness*, Mark Taylor

○ ⌀ 161 *Off the Radar*, Brian Carter + Annette LeCuyer